better assess his theological-philosophical contribution and expose the human qualities lying behind his more abstract formulations.

DAVID H. HOPPER is Associate Professor in the Religion Department of Macalester College, St. Paul, Minnesota. He grew up in New Jersey, received his B.A. from Yale, then returned to New Jersey where he obtained the B.D. degree from Princeton Theological Seminary in 1953. After studying for a year in Bonn, Germany, he again returned to Princeton where he received the Th.D. degree in 1959. That fall he moved to St. Paul and Macalester College. He has served as an exchange professor at Lane College, Jackson, Tennessee.

# TILLICH: a theological portrait

# TILLICH:

J. B. LIPPINCOTT COMPANY

# a theological portrait
# by David Hopper

Philadelphia and New York
*1968*

First Edition
Copyright © 1967 by David H. Hopper
Printed in the United States of America
Library of Congress Catalog Card No. 68-10618

*To*
*My Father and Mother*

# CONTENTS

*Introduction* .......................... 9

I Formative Influences .................. 15

II The Controversy with Barth ............ 35

III The Hirsch Affair—and After .......... 65

IV The Ontological Frame of Reference ..... 101

V Exposition of the *Systematic Theology* .... 127

VI "Artist's" Postscript ................... 170

*Index* ................................ 187

# INTRODUCTION

This book on the life and thought of Paul Johannes Tillich (1886–1965) is an effort to offer a summary view of the man and his work, an over-all analysis and assessment, as it were. As such it undertakes a task that thus far has not been attempted and that needs to be done. There has been, of course, no lack of technical works written about aspects and phases of Tillich's thought, but no serious effort, I think, has yet been made to offer an overview of the man and his thought, one that has in mind an audience wider than that of the Tillich specialist.

However, this book is designed to go beyond mere analysis of Tillich's thought in an effort to convey some of the excitement and fire of that thought in the process of its expression. I have accordingly called it a portrait rather than an assessment or an analysis. In the world of art, a world so close to Tillich's heart, a good portrait often is able to capture the personality and inner spirit of the subject in a way that a photograph generally fails to do. If ever there were need of—or if there is room for—such a thing as a theological portrait, I believe Paul Tillich represents a prime first subject. For no man sought more earnestly to speak to his time, and yet no man's thought—in

9

our generation at least—is more in danger of becoming the private preserve of the pedant and academician.

This is partly Tillich's fault. In his interpretation of the philosophical-theological task, he strongly espoused the idea of creative, conceptual innovation.[1] And, in line with his concept of the creative role of the systematician, he shaped a philosophical-theological idiom that in its strangeness and novelty worked against his purpose of speaking to and for his time. As a result, Tillich's published English works bear a certain mystifying quality for many interested American readers. They instill in the reader a sense of uncertainty about the final meaning of his fundamental words and concepts. The result has been that for many Tillich has taken on something of the fascination of the unknown, and at times he has been granted a stature that seems larger than life. He often appears to stand apart from us rather than mix with us in the common course of life. Some have actually seemed to *want* to put him beyond reach—and keep him there as an idol of profundity. I do not want to deny Tillich's profundity, but I *do* want to emphasize that Tillich's own major purpose was to address life and that he was a man among men.

Therefore I offer the following theological portrait —a picture of the man and his thought that, though not neglecting the scholarly task, seeks to accent the bond of life and thought that is the mark of one who claimed to be an existential thinker. To accomplish

1. This is especially apparent in the definition of "Systematik" in Tillich's earlier writings, *Das System der Wissenschaften nach Gegenständen und Methoden,* and "Religionsphilosophie"; cf. *Gesammelte Werke,* (Stuttgart: Evangelisches Verlagswerk, 1959), I, 223-224, 315-316.

this purpose I have sought to allow Tillich to speak for himself. I have tried to show how Tillich viewed patterns of his own life, and I offer descriptions of certain key life situations in which he was involved. Since portraiture can easily turn into caricature, I hope that by allowing Tillich and others to present themselves this danger can be minimized—even though such an approach runs the risk of a somewhat episodic treatment. If the reader, however, can be brought to experience the vitality of theological debate and develop an appreciation for Tillich's philosophical formulations, the risk is well worth taking. Actually, where I as portraitist play the artist—and where the danger of caricature is most acute—is in the selection of the theological encounters and philosophical-theological statements that are offered as significant and especially expressive of the man and his thought.

In general I have tried to move from the easier aspects of Tillich's life-thought to the more difficult. In the opening chapter I have simply brought together material supplied by Tillich on the early, formative influences in his life. The sources for this opening phase of the portrait are readily available to English readers, but I have chosen to underline in this particular collation the revolutionary-romantic motif that Tillich himself designated as distinctive of his life and work. This dual theme of revolution and romanticism finds signal embodiment in Tillich's doctrine of the kairos, his most distinctive and widely known philosophical-theological concept from the early 1920's through to the late 1940's. A brief exposition of this doctrine provides the necessary background for two vital theological encounters that follow.

In Chapter II, "The Controversy with Barth," Tillich takes issue with Karl Barth, probably the modern era's most forceful advocate of traditional and neo-traditional theological thought. What begins as a somewhat sticky discussion of the nature of dialectics evolves into a clear parting of the ways between Tillich who wants to universalize the faith through romantic identification with the movement of history and culture and Barth who wants to carry on the theological task within the framework of traditional Christian categories and realities—God, the Canon, the Church. Tillich, having already announced the kairos doctrine, steadfastly affirmed this program as a theological alternative to that of Barth.

Chapter III, "The Hirsch Affair—and After," is in part an exploration of the viability of Tillich's alternative, the difficulties and theoretical problems encountered in its formulation, and the additions and corrections Tillich felt necessary in the midst of the personal and historical crisis that was the Hirsch affair. As an important offshoot of this presentation, there emerges evidence for identifying the one major shift in Tillich's thought.

Only in passing, and independent of the portrait itself, it might be pointed out that Chapters II and III, taken together, sketch in background vital to an understanding of present-day theological patterns by which younger theologians are attempting again to recast and radically reformulate Christian doctrine on the basis of an intuitive reading of the times and what they feel the times demand theologically. It matters little whether the cue is taken from Tillich or from Bonhoeffer and a world come of age, essentially the program is the same—though without the disciplined philosophical grounding—as that proposed more than four decades ago by Tillich. Barth's alternative also remains—the assertion that there was a time in the spiritual life of men more important than our own and that to theologize responsibly in this faith is to speak also of Church and Canon.

Though the kairos doctrine and Religious Socialism were uniquely expressive of the important revolutionary-romantic motif in Tillich's life, there lies behind the idea of kairos an ontological frame of reference, a certain philosophical view of reality, that is essential to understanding Tillich as a thinker. In Chapter IV explication of this philosophical frame of reference is presented in the form of an analysis of Tillich's seriously neglected 1912 treatise, *Mysticism and Guiltconsciousness in Schelling's Philosophical Development*.[2] And then in Chapter V, the decisive significance of this 1912 treatise is elaborated through application of its central categories and ideas to an exposition of the *Systematic Theology*, Tillich's *magnum opus* of the years 1951–63. Although it must be anticipated that in these two chapters the reader may suffer a loss of existential involvement, this ideational foundation is absolutely essential to comprehending both the man and his work. The two chapters together represent an attempt to offer a major simplification of Tillich's thought, certainly one of the most difficult tasks confronted by any Tillich interpreter.

2. *Mystik und Schuldbewusstsein in Schellings philosophischer Entwicklung*, first published in *Beiträge zur Förderung christlicher Theologie*, (Gütersloh: Bertelsmann, 1912), XVI, No. I.

The final chapter, "'Artist's' Postscript," is a presentation of the author's own interpretation of the portrait, a discussion and assessment of Tillich's theological contribution. It should be understood that this postscript is not intended to preclude other interpretations of the same portrait by readers who see with different eyes. That others *may see* with different eyes is a further advantage and challenge of this mode of presentation.

# I

## FORMATIVE INFLUENCES

In three separate places, Paul Tillich set down in writing personal accounts and reminiscences of his life and the development of his thought.[1] These accounts are especially valuable aids to an understanding of both the man and his thought. They provide important insights into the formative influences of his life. They also reveal the manner in which Tillich himself understood and interpreted his life.

1. *The Interpretation of History*, (New York: Charles Scribner's Sons, 1936), pp. 3–73; *The Protestant Era* (Chicago: University of Chicago Press, 1948), pp. ix-xxix; and the volume edited by Charles W. Kegley and Robert W. Bretall, *The Theology of Paul Tillich*, (New York: The Macmillan Co., 1952), pp. 3–21. Fr. George F. Tavard suggests also the Tillich article "The Conquest of Intellectual Provincialism: Europe and America" (1953), republished in *Theology of Culture*, (New York: Oxford University Press, 1959), pp. 159–176; but this article is of minor significance in comparison with the other pieces.

One certainly cannot by-pass this material if one would come to a meaningful understanding of Tillich's thought. But, at the same time, there is reason to urge that a measure of caution be used in assessing and evaluating these accounts; for it seems that Tillich does not always present a fully consistent picture of the development of aspects of his thought and work. It is only natural that Tillich should have been more concerned with the philosophical questions, with what might be termed the universal truths, than with particular details of historical sequence. It is probably true of any great thinker. Major intellectual concerns have a tendency at times to shade the picture of the past. Because of this, use of Tillich's reminiscences should also be weighed against his own early writings. Illustration of the need for caution should be given at the start.

Writing in the Kegley and Bretall volume in 1952, Tillich stated that with his acceptance of a theological professorship in Marburg in 1924 he

> . . . met the first radical effects of the neo-ortho-
> dox theology on theological students: cultural
> problems were excluded from theological
> thought; theologians like Schleiermacher, Har-
> nack, Troeltsch, Otto were contemptuously re-
> jected: social and political ideas were banned
> from theological discussions. The contrast with
> the experiences in Berlin was overwhelming, at
> first depressing and then inciting: a new way had
> to be found. In Marburg, in 1925, I began work

on my *Systematic Theology*, the first volume of which appeared in 1951.[2]

This statement seems to suggest that disagreement with major aspects of the thought of Karl Barth and the impact of neo-orthodox thought upon students was what impelled Tillich to seek "a new way" and to begin work on his *Systematic Theology* in the year 1925. If such is the meaning of this passage—and it is difficult to interpret it in any other way—then statements by Tillich in some of his other writings tend to confuse the picture. For example, in the introduction to the third volume of the *Systematic Theology* he states that it was at Marburg in *1924* that he began work on his system and that this was an outgrowth of regular classroom lectures in the field of systematic theology. At still another place, however, in the Introduction to *The Protestant Era*, Tillich writes:

> I have traveled a long way to my present theological position, a way that started in my first larger book, *Das System der Wissenschaften nach Gegenstanden und Methoden*. . . . In many respects the ideas developed in this book have determined my thinking up to the present moment, especially those on biology, technical sciences, history, and metaphysics. Theology is defined as "theonomous metaphysics," a definition that was a first and rather insufficient step toward what I now call the "method of correlation."[3]

2. Kegley and Bretall, p. 14.
3. *The Protestant Era*, p. xxvi.

The work referred to in this quotation was published in 1923, some time before Tillich's Marburg experience—a year that also saw a sharp exchange of views between Tillich and Barth, an exchange to be described in detail below. What becomes apparent as one studies Tillich's 1923 writings is that his views were already quite distinctive and deeply held well before Marburg and 1925. Furthermore, there is reason to believe that in 1923 he was already quite committed to the idea of a system as the appropriate form of his own creative thought—at least a reading of *The System of the Sciences According to Their Objects and Methods*[4] leaves one with this distinct impression. More perhaps could be said on the matter of the "why" and the "when" of initiation of work on the *Systematic Theology*, but this would go beyond our purpose, which is simply to point out the importance of weighing Tillich's autobiographical reflections against the course of his substantive thought wherever this is possible.

If in some particulars a sort of guarded scepticism is advisable, at another point full and ready acceptance is prescribed. Writing in 1949, in an article for *The Christian Century*, Tillich declared: "A few great and lasting things are decisive for the human mind, and . . . to cling to them is more important than to look for dramatic changes."[5] Of far greater significance for

4. *Das System der Wissenschaften nach Gegenständen und Methoden* (Göttingen: Vandenhoeck and Ruprecht, 1923).

5. "Beyond Religious Socialism: How My Mind Has Changed in the Last Decade," *The Christian Century*, (June 15, 1949), LXVI, 733. Writing in the Introduction to *The Protestant Era*, Tillich also notes: " . . . more obvious than the changes from the earlier to the more recent articles in

an understanding of Tillich's thought than precise details of chronology is this reflection by Tillich upon the course of his own lifework. It is this statement that will constitute the climax of our exposition and interpretation. On the way to this goal, however, we have first to meet a man who experienced deeply the course of life, its joys and challenges, its triumphs and defeats, who lived a vital, creative life. Let us turn to consider some of the formative influences in that life as Tillich himself described them.

*　　*　　*

Paul Tillich was born on August 20, 1886, in the small village of Starzeddel, in the province of Brandenburg in eastern Germany. His father was pastor of the village church, but within a few years he was asked to become superintendent of the diocese of Schönfliess-Neumark in the same province. The father held this position for about ten years before being called to Berlin around 1900 to fill an important administrative post within the Prussian Territorial Church.

About these early years Tillich makes a number of interesting observations. He speaks of a certain romanticism instilled within him. Living close to the country in eastern Germany, he developed a strong feeling for nature:

---

this collection is the continuity of the main line of thought and the permanence of the basic principles. It sometimes strikes me (and this is probably a very common experience), when I read some of my earliest writings, how much of what I believed to be a recent achievement is already explicitly or at least implicitly contained in them." (*The Protestant Era,* pp. x-xi).

19

. . . my tie with the country lies [deep] in my soul. Nearly all great memories, and all strong longings are interlaced with landscapes, with the soil and with weather, with corn fields, and the smell of autumnal potato foliage, with the forms of clouds, with wind, flowers and woods. On all my later journeys, too, through Germany and through southern and western Europe, the impressions of the land were the strongest.[6]

The sea also made a deep impression upon the young Tillich:

Most important, however, was the fact that from my eighth year onward annually I spent some weeks, later even months, by the seaside. The experience of the infinite bordering upon the finite, as one has it by the sea . . . supplied my imagination with a symbol from which feeling could win substance[7] . . . the yearly escape to the Baltic Sea, with its limitless horizon, was the great event, the flight into the open, into unrestricted space. That I have chosen a place at the Atlantic Ocean for the days of my retirement is certainly due to these early experiences.[8]

This fascination, this sense of identity with nature, prepared him in later years for "the tremendous emotional impact" of Schelling's philosophy of nature,

6. *The Interpretation of History*, p. 7.
7. *Ibid.*, p. 7.
8. Kegley and Bretall, p. 6.

though Tillich also says that he was, at the same time, "aware that this philosophy was scientifically impossible."[9]

The romanticism imbibed by Tillich during his early days was not limited to nature. It embraced also a "feeling for the past." To be sure, life in the small medieval towns that he knew as a youth was often confining and restrictive. These towns represented "a small, protected, and self-contained world." The countryside and the seaside by contrast were open, expansive, inviting. And yet these same towns stood witness to the past and provided Tillich with a sense of participation in the centuries of struggle and accomplishment that made his own days what they were. As he expressed it: "To grow up in towns in which every stone is witness of a period many centuries past produces a feeling for history, not as a matter of knowledge, but as a living reality in which the past participates in the present."[10] The sense of sharing life with the past added depth to Tillich's awareness of the present, enlarged the meaning of time.

Along with the physical environment, social and educational conditions figured large in the molding of the young Tillich. The provincial class structure fostered in him an unease which later matured into a deep concern for the depressed and alienated segments of society. Tillich suggests that it was during his early training in the common school that he first became aware of class frictions. He found that his sympathies rather naturally inclined to the lower

9. *Ibid.*, p. 4.
10. *Ibid.*, p. 5.

classes, against the *bourgeoisie* and upper classes, even though as son of the town pastor he was included within the latter.[11]

To this social aspect of Tillich's early schooling must be added the actual content of instruction as a factor shaping his later interests. With enrollment in a *Gymnasium* around the age of twelve, he was introduced to the traditions of Greek culture and learning. Though he had been privately tutored in Latin at an earlier age, Tillich was especially attracted to the study of classical Greek, and he eagerly pursued these studies at a second *Gymnasium* in Berlin, when his father was subsequently transferred to that city. Of this stage in his intellectual development, Tillich wrote: "My love of the Greek language was a vehicle for my love of the Greek culture and especially the early Greek philosophies. One of my most enthusiastically prepared and best received courses had as its subject matter the pre-Socratic philosophy."[12] This interest led in turn to active inquiry into the whole field of philosophy. And thus, by the time he entered the University of Berlin, some three or four years later, Tillich possessed "a good knowledge of the history of philosophy, and a basic acquaintance with Kant and Fichte."[13]

The growing interest in philosophy played an important role not only in Tillich's intellectual development, but also in the process of his maturation.

11. *Interpretation of History*, pp. 8–9.
12. Kegley and Bretall, p. 9: cf. *Interpretation of History*, pp. 17–18.
13. Kegley and Bretall, p. 10; cf. *Interpretation of History*, pp. 30–31.

22

Though the formative influences of the physical environment, the social and educational factors, were no doubt very important, the matter of his relationship to his parents was undoubtedly most basic. Both his parents, he says,

> . . . were strong personalities. My father was a conscientious, very dignified, completely convinced and, in the presence of doubt, angry supporter of the conservative Lutheran point of view. My mother, coming from the more democratic and liberal Rhineland, did not have the authoritarian attitude. She was, however, deeply influenced by the rigid morals of Western Reformed Protestantism. The consequence was a restrictive pressure in thought as well as in action, in spite (and partly because) of a warm atmosphere of loving care.[14]

In *The Interpretation of History*, however, Tillich refers to the "early death of my mother,"[15] and later on in the same work he indicates that a major struggle for personal independence centered in his relationship with his father:

> My father's authority, which was at once personal and intellectual, and which because of his position in the Church, coincided for me with the religious authority of revelation, made every manifestation of autonomous thinking a piece of religious daring, and involved the critique of authority in a sense of guilt. The immemorial

14. Kegley and Bretall, p. 8.
15. *Interpretation of History*, p. 4.

experience of mankind, that new knowledge can be won only through breaking a taboo, that all autonomous thinking is accompanied by a consciousness of guilt, has been a fundamental experience of my own life."[16]

Tillich's attempts to establish independence from his father were hampered "by the unavoidable guilt consciousness produced by the identification of the parental with the divine authority."[17] But here his interest in philosophy played a crucial, liberating role. Through discussions with his father he was finally able to arrive at a philosophical position over-against his father, a position that he was able to maintain steadfastly. In this way he came to experience his first real measure of personal autonomy. It represented a major turning point in Tillich's life and helped to fix in him a lifelong pattern of thought. Though he refers to these philosophical discussions with his father as "the most happy instances of a positive relation to my father," Tillich goes on to say:

> Nevertheless, in these discussions the break-through occurred. From an independent philosophical position a state of independence spread out into all directions, theoretically first, practically later. It is this difficult and painful break-through to autonomy which has made me immune against any system of thought or life which demands the surrender of this autonomy."[18]

16. *Ibid.*, pp. 22–23.
17. Kegley and Bretall, p. 8.
18. *Ibid.*, p. 8.

In summing up the experiences of his early years, Tillich discerned two powerful motives at work: the romantic and the revolutionary. The romantic motive stirred in him feelings of identification, feelings of "at-oneness," with the natural order, with the past, with the logos of the philosophical tradition. The revolutionary motive on the other hand prompted him to oppose all patterns of authority and privilege that threatened to stay the surge of life. He concluded: "The balance of these motives has remained the basic problem of my life ever since."[19]

Certainly one can observe the presence of these motives in the patterns of thought that emerged during the years of Tillich's university education. Philosophical interests continued to play a fundamental role in his academic endeavors, although a basic theological concern was also present.[20] To his earlier knowledge of Greek philosophy, of Kant and Fichte, was added an appreciation for Schleiermacher, Hegel, and Schelling, the latter becoming especially important for him and constituting the subject of study for two advanced degrees.[21] Schleiermacher's theology of "feeling," Hegel's philosophy of "spirit," and Schelling's philosophy of "freedom" all bear vital, emotional dimensions consistent with the romantic spirit. In a more formal philosophical sense all of these men stood as advocates of the "principle of identity," an essential element in any systematic statement of the "romantic" point of view. We shall have occasion to discuss the principle

19. *Ibid.*, p. 9.
20. *Ibid.*, p. 10.
21. Doctor of Philosophy and Licentiate of Theology; *Ibid.*, p. 10.

of identity in more detail later.[22] It is enough simply to point out here that Tillich's developing philosophical concerns involved a deep feeling both for nature and history, a reflection of the sensitivities of his earliest years.

As for the "revolutionary motive," this is a somewhat easier motif to trace through Tillich's student years. He spoke, for example, of his theological studies under Martin Kaehler at Halle, studies that contributed to Tillich's later formulation of the "Protestant principle." Kaehler's particular contribution was to provide Tillich with a new appreciation for the Reformation doctrine of "justification by faith," or "justification through faith" as Tillich very much preferred to describe it. He said of Kaehler and the development of his own thought during this time:

> Under his influence a group of advanced students and younger professors developed the new understanding of the Protestant principle in different ways. The step I myself made in these years was the insight that the principle of justification through faith refers not only to the religious-ethical but also to the religious-intellectual life. Not only he who is in sin but also he who is in doubt is justified through faith. The situation of doubt, even of doubt about God, need not separate us from God. There is faith in every serious doubt; namely, the faith in the truth as such, even if the only truth we can express is our lack of truth . . . he who doubts in such an at-

22. See Chapter IV below.

titude is "justified" in his thinking. So the paradox got hold of me that he who seriously denies God, affirms Him. . . . There is, I soon realized, no place *beside* the divine, there is no possible atheism, there is no wall between the religious and the non-religious. The holy embraces both itself and the secular.[23]

As the Reformation doctrine of justification became the basis for a revolutionary attack upon a religion of "works-righteousness," so Tillich saw in his own extension of the doctrine a radical critique of the forms of orthodox belief. "Good works of the mind," he asserted, were no more determinative of the Christian life than were "works of the law."

Expression of the freedom achieved with this insight is seen in Tillich's readiness to defend, within the context of Christian faith, the theoretical question of the possible nonexistence of the historical Jesus. He initially presented this viewpoint after the completion of his work on his doctoral degree and before the submission of his dissertation for the degree of Licentiate of Theology. He writes on the point as follows:

An authoritative proof for my development are those theses, presented during Whitsuntide in

23. *The Protestant Era*, p. xiv-xv. It might be well to note at this point that the extension of the idea of "justification through faith" to the intellectual realm is accomplished by means of the principle of the "coincidence of opposites." In asserting the presence of faith in the midst of doubt Tillich is actually making use of this logical principle. At times he shows a tendency to equate this principle with "justification through faith" itself; cf. *Interpretation of History*, pp. 172–

1911, to a group of theological friends, in which I raised and attempted to answer the question, how the Christian doctrine might be understood, if the non-existence of the historical Jesus should become historically probable. Even today [i.e. in 1936], I maintain the radicalism of this question over against compromises. . . . The foundation of Christian belief is not the historical Jesus but the biblical picture of Christ.[24]

That Tillich in his theological thought had clearly broken free from the usual patterns of Christian belief is further confirmed in a pamphlet published in 1915, under the lengthy title *The Concept of the Supernatural, Its Dialectical Character, and the Principle of Identity, Represented in the Supranatural Theology Before Schleiermacher.*[25] In this work Tillich rejected the traditional concept of God as "a being beside other beings," and expressed preference for a dialectical conception transcending the subject-object cleavage. Here already Tillich was speaking of "the God above God."[26]

The critical, revolutionary character of this phase of Tillich's thought had roots not only in his theological studies under Kaehler, but also in his analysis of Schelling's philosophy, treated in the dissertations

173, *Systematic Theology* (Chicago: University of Chicago Press, 1963); III, 228. For a fuller discussion of the coincidence of opposites, see below, pp. 41–42, 112–113.

24. *Interpretation of History*, pp. 33–34.

25. *Der Begriff des Uebernatürlichen, sein dialektischer Charakter und das Prinzip der Identität, dargestellt an der supranaturalistischen Theologie vor Schleiermacher.* (Königsberg: Madrasch, 1915).

26. *Der Begriff des Uebernatürlichen* . . . , p. 44.

of 1910 and 1912. Tillich is quite explicit on this point:

> The relation of these fundamental thoughts of theology to my philosophical development was determined, first of all, by the work of Schelling, particularly the ideas of his later period. I thought that, fundamentally, I had found the union of theology and philosophy in the philosophical explanation of the Christian doctrine through the older Schelling, in his founding of a Christian philosophy of existence in contrast to Hegel's humanistic philosophy of essence and in his interpretation of history as the History of Salvation. I must confess, that even today, I find more "theonomous philosophy" in Schelling than in any of the other idealists. But to be sure, not even Schelling was able to bring about a unity of theology and philosophy.[27]

The last assertion in the above quotation, that "not even Schelling was able to bring about a unity of theology and philosophy," was a conviction that Tillich seems to have come to as a result of his experience in World War I. Following the conclusion of his theological studies in 1912, Tillich served briefly as assistant pastor in parishes of the Old Prussian United Church, and then, with the outbreak of World War I, he enlisted as a chaplain in the German Army and served in that capacity from September 1914 to September 1918. His description of his war experience reflects significant disillusionment:

27. *Interpretation of History*, p. 35.

The first weeks had not passed before one's original enthusiasm disappeared; after a few months I became convinced that the war would last indefinitely and ruin all Europe. Above all, I saw that the unity of the first weeks was an illusion, that the nation was split into classes, and that the industrial masses considered the Church as an unquestioned ally of the ruling groups. This situation became more and more manifest toward the end of the war. It produced the revolution, in which the imperial Germany collapsed.[28]

It was exposure to the tragedy of war and its aftermath that brought Tillich to an awareness of inadequacies in Schelling's philosophy of history and an appreciation for what Tillich described as the "abyss" of existence, the feeling of meaninglessness and despair:

The World War in my own experience was the catastrophe of idealistic thinking in general. Even Schelling's philosophy was drawn into this catastrophe. The chasm, which without doubt, Schelling had seen, but soon had covered up again, opened itself. The experience of the four years of war tore this chasm open for me and for my entire generation to such an extent that it was impossible ever to cover it up. If a reunion of theology and philosophy should again become possible, it could be achieved only in such a way as would do justice to this experience of the abyss of our existence.[29]

28. Kegley and Bretall, p. 12.
29. *Interpretation of History*, p. 35.

30

It must be emphasized that World War I did not mark, for Tillich, any sort of radical or complete break with the thought of Schelling. Rather, it represented only the need for a modification of Schelling's philosophy of history. This modification took the form of a deeper appreciation of the reality of tragedy and the necessity of historical struggle and reflected the influence of Marx and Nietzsche. The basic lines however of a dynamic ontology, an ontology affirming both being and becoming as worked out before World War I, were clearly preserved.[30] What emerged from the war experience was a new realization of the potentialities of destructiveness, as well as creativity, within the historical order. Tillich offers confirmation of this interpretation:

> History became the central problem of my theology and philosophy because of the historical reality as I found it when I returned from the first World War: a chaotic Germany and Europe; the end of the period of the victorious *bourgeoisie* and of the nineteenth-century way of life; the split between the Lutheran churches and the proletariat; the gap between the transcendent message of traditional Christianity and the immanent hopes of the revolutionary movements. The situation demanded interpretation as well as action.[31]

Interpretation and action were combined in the founding and organization of the German Religious-

30. See Chapter IV below.
31. *The Protestant Era*, p. xvii.

Socialist movement. Tillich took part in organizing this movement immediately after the war and became one of its leading spokesmen. A politically oriented group, made up primarily, it seems, of scholarly people, the Religious Socialists sought to provide a meaningful interpretation of the times and acted to further the ends of justice and reform in society at large. The extent of the revolutionary fervor of the group is indicated by its endorsement of much of Marxist thought, but the really distinctive feature of Religious Socialism, and that which clearly marked it off from the mainstream of Marxism, was the rejection of utopianism and the espousal instead of Tillich's concept of the kairos.[32]

The doctrine of the kairos, as enunciated by Tillich after World War I, was, for many years, one of his most creative and influential constructs. It constituted the center around which most of Tillich's thought and writings revolved in the two decades after the war. As indicated in the third volume of the *Systematic Theology*, it continued, to the end, to find a place in his systematic thought. In essence the doctrine of the kairos is closely bound up with the Protestant principle that Tillich had begun to formulate before World War I. It is in the idea of the kairos, in fact, that the Protestant principle comes to its most forceful expression. As the Protestant principle rejected every human claim in the face of God, so the kairos concept denied to the structures and forms of the social-political order all claims of absoluteness. Tillich maintained that none of the historical-cultural forms

32. See Eduard Heimann, "Tillich's Doctrine of Religious Socialism," Kegley and Bretall, *op cit.*, pp. 312–25.

in which man expresses his spiritual being can claim finality. They all bear a limited temporal validity. Periodically, Tillich argued, they come into crisis and are replaced by new structures of meaning arising out of the historical process. Just as the Protestant principle is grace as well as judgment (God's affirmation of man in spite of man's sinfulness), so the kairos represents the emergence of new forms of meaning and life amidst the death of the old. These new forms of life are not really predictable but arise out of the ambiguous depths of the historical situation and provide a new being for society as a whole. A kairos thus represents a moment in the over-all process of history in which a turning takes place. The old is either abandoned or transformed, and new possibilities of life are actualized in all areas of culture and society, in the aesthetic as well as in the social-political realm.[33] In the kairos doctrine trenchant expression was given both to revolutionary protest and to romantic identification with the new spiritual forces believed to be emerging in history.

It was around this idea of the kairos that the Religious-Socialist movement developed. Tillich and his colleagues believed that a kairos was at hand in the postwar situation of central Europe. And thus, in the course of subsequent years, they worked for the realization of a "theonomous" culture, a "new" culture in which the open breach between the religious and the secular orders would be closed. Consistent with the insight from his university years that right-

33. Cf. *The Protestant Era*, pp. 200–205. The original statement of the kairos idea, in translation, is found in *The Protestant Era*, pp. 32–51.

eousness was to be known in the midst of doubt, Tillich affirmed the positive, religious meaning to be found in the midst of a situation of political and social chaos.

Such then are some of the broad lines in the development of Tillich's early thought. Many factors led into the formulation of the kairos concept. Certainly from his early days one can note in Tillich's spiritual development a rejection of the parochial interest in favor of the more inclusive, the affirmation of freedom over-against authoritarian restriction, and a preference for the dynamic qualities of life over the static. Expression of all of these concerns and forceful affirmation of the kairos doctrine are to be found in a significant exchange of views with Karl Barth in the year 1923. Chiefly to be seen in this exchange, however, is Tillich's revolt against traditional theological categories and formulations, a revolt first manifested before World War I during Tillich's student days. The debate with Barth is worthy of careful recapitulation. Though it does not spell out in detail all of the philosophical presuppositions that inspired Tillich's attack, it affords significant illustration of the revolutionary-romantic spirit that gripped Tillich and led him into conflict with the leading figure in the postwar theological renascence.

# II

## The Controversy with Barth

The belief, current among Tillich and others in the German Religious-Socialist movement, that special meaning adhered to the times of World War I and its aftermath found numerous forms of confirmation. The postwar years were a period of great social, political, and intellectual ferment. Tillich described these years as he knew them in Germany:

The political problems determined our whole existence; even after revolution and inflation they were matters of life and death. The social structure was in a state of dissolution; the human relations with respect to authority, education, family, sex, friendship, and pleasure were in a creative chaos. Revolutionary art came into the foreground, supported by the Republic, attacked by the majority of the people. Psychoanalytic ideas spread and produced a consciousness of realities which had been carefully repressed in previous generations. The participation in these movements created manifold problems, conflicts, fears, expectations, ecstasies, and despairs, practically as well as theoretically.[1]

What was perhaps most clear was that an old order was passing. But what was much less clear was the positive meaning of the times and the determination of the direction of the future. The Religious-Socialist movement was, of course, founded to meet precisely this need. It represented, however, only one among numerous alternatives. A great variety of programs and conflicting ideas formed part of the "creative chaos" of postwar Europe.

Within the theological world the picture of new and conflicting views was much the same as that which existed in society at large. The year 1919 affords illustration. In that year Tillich began the formulation of his theology of history with a brief, provocative treatise entitled, "Concerning the Idea of a Theology of Culture."[2] In this treatise his earlier understanding of the Protestant principle found expression in the thesis that religion was not a special sector or province within culture but a factor pervading all of culture, a thesis that Tillich maintained to the end of his life. By way of contrast, however, in that same year, Karl Barth, a young German-Swiss

1. Kegley and Bretall, pp. 13–14.
2. "Ueber die Idee einer Theologie der Kultur," *Religionsphilosophie der Kultur*. (Berlin: Reuther and Reichard, 1919).

36

theologian, proposed a very different understanding of the relationship of faith and culture. Barth's thesis was presented in the form of a theological commentary on the letter of Paul to the Romans and was published under the simple title, *The Epistle to the Romans*.[3] He argued that God stood in judgment over-against the world of sinful man, that God was absolutely free vis-à-vis His creation, and that this freedom of God was uniquely expressed in His gracious revelation in Christ Jesus. Man's creativity, man's cultural achievements and potentialities were not for Barth, as they were for Tillich, a means of salvation; nor could they provide a basis for a synthesis of the Word of God and the wisdom of this world. For Barth, judgment pointed man away from himself, away from man's world, to the reality of God in Christ as witnessed to in the Scriptures.

Although there was a strong accent upon judgment in the thought of both Tillich and Barth—both inveighed strongly against modern forms of idolatry— it was clear that beyond judgment the two men moved in quite different directions. Barth pointed to God, the One who was other than man, the One who in Christ offered man forgiveness. Tillich, on the other hand, pointed to the possibilities of new creation that were to be found in the contemporary historical situation, possibilities existing alongside the destruction and decay of old structures of meaning. For Tillich, God was not "a being" other than man. God was a dimension of reality transcending the subject-object

3. *Der Römerbrief* (Bern: G. A. Bäschlin, 1919); English translation by Edwyn C. Hoskyns from the sixth German edition (London: Oxford Univ. Press, 1933).

cleavage and expressive of both judgment and grace in every present moment.

Tillich and Barth consistently developed these divergent lines of thought following 1919. It is clear that Barth did not alter the direction of his thought concerning the freedom and personhood of God except to move increasingly away from certain earlier philosophical dependencies (Plato, Kant, Kierkegaard) towards a more Biblical and church-oriented theology. As for Tillich there is no evidence to indicate that Barth's strongly-voiced polemic against the syncretistic, liberal theological tradition had any great effect upon the patterns of *his* thought. Quite the contrary. From 1919 until 1924, during his years as "Privatdozent" of theology at the University of Berlin, Tillich pursued his interest in a theology of culture. He "lectured on subjects which included the relation of religion to politics, art, philosophy, depth psychology, and sociology."[4] During these years also he apparently became personally acquainted with Ernst Troeltsch, one of the leading figures in the religious-historical school (*Religionsgeshichtlicheschule*) of theological thought. Tillich identified closely with phases of Troeltsch's thought,[5] and when Troeltsch died prematurely in 1923, Tillich significantly dedicated the major work, *The System of the Sciences According to Their Objects and Methods*, to Troeltsch's memory. In the light of these facts, it is

4. Kegley and Bretall, p. 13.
5. Cf. Kurt Herberger, "Historismus und Kairos, Die Ueberwindung des Historismus bei Ernst Troeltsch und Paul Tillich" (I Teil: Ernst Troeltsch, II Teil: Paul Tillich), *Theologische Blätter*, XIV (1935), 129–41, 161–75.

difficult to believe that Tillich did not deeply sym-
pathize with Troeltsch's 1921 criticism of the theological views of Friedrich Gogarten, an early supporter of Barth's dialectical or neo-orthodox
theology.[6] And it is not at all surprising that Tillich
should have been invited in the course of time to spell
out in greater detail his own differences with Barth and
Gogarten.[7] This invitation was extended to Tillich in
1923 by Karl Ludwig Schmidt, editor of the influential theological journal, *Theologische Blätter*. Tillich
accepted the invitation and offered in that periodical
a thoroughgoing criticism of Barth's theological position. Gogarten's name figured prominently in the
critique, but it was clear that Barth was the primary
target. The title of Tillich's article was: "Critical and
Positive Paradox: A Statement of Views in Opposition
to Karl Barth and Friedrich Gogarten."[8]

6. Ernst Troeltsch, "Ein Apfel vom Baume Kierkegaards,"
*Die christliche Welt*, XXXV (1921), 186–90. See also Til-
lich's own criticism of Barth in his article "Kairos," *Die Tat*,
XIV, (1922), 335–36.

7. Fr. Tavard's analysis of Tillich's early relationship with
Barth is not correct. Especially questionable is his interpretation of Barth's early thought. Cf. George Tavard, *Paul Tillich and the Christian Message*, (New York: Charles Scribner's Sons, 1962) p. 11. For the development of Barth's
thought, see Thomas F. Torrance, *Karl Barth, An Introduction to His Early Theology*, 1910–1931 (London: SCM Press,
1962). In my judgment, J. Heywood Thomas is wrong in his
suggestion that Tillich's "early thought" was at one time
"full . . . of Barthian ideas." Cf. J. Heywood Thomas, *Paul
Tillich: An Appraisal*, (Philadelphia: Westminster Press,
1963), p. 18. For further discussion of this matter see below,
p. 79 n. 26.

8. "Kritisches und positives Paradox: Eine Auseinandersetz-
ung mit Karl Barth und Friedrich Gogarten." *Theologische
Blätter*, (1923), II, 263–69.

A description of the substance of Tillich's criticism of Barth, Barth's reply to Tillich, and Tillich's concluding answer provides insight into aspects of Tillich's clearly independent theological-philosophical position at this stage in the development of his thought. What opens as a rather complex critique by Tillich of Barth's theological method ends up in a delineation of two different theological programs, Tillich arguing for the determinative character for theology of the cultural break between one historical era that was passing and a new one that he believed was dawning, Barth arguing for a differentiation between God and man, Church and world, throughout the course of every era.

*　　*　　*

The first step in Tillich's "exchange of views" with Barth and Gogarten is the designation of a difference in the understanding of the nature of the dialectic that Tillich and Barth separately use in their appraisal of the human situation vis-à-vis God. This difference is implicit in Tillich's contrast of the terms "critical" and "positive" paradox.[9] In Tillich's eyes Barth's negative or critical dialectic, the rejection of all human pretension and idolatry, derives from a fixed point and place in time. For Tillich this can only mean that this dialectic lacks a ground in the Unconditional; it is itself a part of the world of the conditional and the particular, and therefore stands in danger of idolatry. Tillich writes:

> An immediate, unparadoxical relationship to the Unconditional which is not inclusive of the per-

9. Cf. *The Protestant Era*, p. xiii.

manent and radical No [of the dialectic] is not a relationship to the Unconditional but to a conditional which makes the claim of being unconditional, that is, to an idol; [as a result] precisely those things and words, such as religion and Bible, Christ and God—especially God—which should express the paradox, are in continuous danger of assuming this idolatrous, undialectical character and of becoming objective and thereby conditional.[10]

Clearly recognizable in this pattern of thought are the lines of Tillich's earlier 1915 criticism of the orthodox, supranatural view of God. This, however, is obviously not an easy world to come to know; and Barth, in his subsequent reply to Tillich, remarks that he, for one, finds it a very strange world with which to come to terms.[11] No doubt a major cause of this puzzlement is the fact that Tillich, in the course of his discussion, makes use of a technical ontological principle that was always one of the fundamental building blocks of his systematic thought, the principle of the coincidence of opposites.[12] It is this principle that largely governs his understanding of "dialectic." The principle as stated by Schelling—though not original with him—is: no matter how sharp the antithesis between two things, a more fundamental moment of identity between the two is always presupposed, because no contrast can be observed or

10. Paul Tillich, "Kritisches und positives Paradox . . . ," *Theologische Blätter;* (Nov. 1923), II, 263.
11. See below, pp. 53–54.
12. See below, Chapter IV.

stated apart from some common ground of comparison. Thus, in Tillich's opening argument, although there is a dimension of *negation* in the relationship of the Unconditional to the conditional (the "abyss of being," in Tillich's more specialized terminology), there is also and always a more basic point of *affirmation* or identity between the two (the "ground of being"). Tillich thus speaks of a "positive paradox" in his analysis of the cultural situation, by which he means that the negative critique of cultural structures and forms is paradoxically and simultaneously grounded in a positive affirmation of life that offers possibilities of new creation. Every moment in history is a moment both of judgment and grace, and it is not possible to have judgment without grace, a point virtually identical with his earlier student-day discovery that one could not have doubt without faith. The basic character of this line of reasoning becomes apparent as Tillich proceeds to criticize Barth's theological views on the relationship of God and nature, God and the human spirit, and God and history.

With regard to God and nature, he notes that Barth and Gogarten reveal a decided aversion to the theological use of the concept of creation. As Tillich interprets their position:

> ... it is better not to speak of the order of creation; it has become, through sin, unrecognizable. What the heathen is able to know of God from nature is only the knowledge of judgment. Even natural science only penetrates deeper into the irrationality of created things.[13]

13. Tillich, "Kritisches und positives Paradox . . . ," 265.

To this Tillich replies by saying that to be able even to speak of the world, or nature, or life as revealing judgment, irrationality, or death is to speak positively of those realities as possessing form and structure. The negative, Tillich asserts, can reveal itself only in the positive.[14] And he then goes on to affirm that:

A look at "the fowls of the air and the lilies of the field" in no way sees only judgment, but also life-creating grace. The 104th Psalm and the song of the angel in the prologue of Goethe's *Faust* stand nearer to this view than that which sees judgment without grace. Certainly the two, judgment and grace, are paradoxical and they open themselves in their paradoxical unity only to the eyes of faith. It is an idolizing Idealism which wants to see grace without judgment, which wants to understand directly and unparadoxically the unity of the Unconditional and the conditional in nature. And it is a demonic Realism which wants to view the destruction of the conditional in nature as a process of nature apart from a paradoxical unity with grace. The one is as impossible as the other, and demonic Realism stands no closer to revelation than does idolizing Idealism.[15]

As a further argument in his rejection of the Barth-Gogarten understanding of the natural order, Tillich makes the observation that in Christian dogmatics the

14. A fundamental theme of Tillich's thought to the end, cf., e.g., *Systematic Theology*, II, p. 86.
15. Tillich, "Kritisches und positives Paradox . . . ," 265.

work of the Trinity, as it relates to the created order, is of a piece—that it is equally the work of the Father, Son, and Holy Spirit. He points out that the New Testament views the Son as a mediator in creation. This means that the order of creation and the order of redemption belong together and that a unitary act of grace is represented in both creation and redemption. Creation is oriented toward redemption and redemption is accomplished within the order of creation. The two are apprehended together in faith.[16]

Tillich then proceeds to discuss the question of the relationship of God and the human spirit and God and history. Both discussions reflect in their separate ways Tillich's use of the same dialectical logic revealed in his discussion of God and nature. In the matter of God and the human spirit, Tillich makes reference to a previous discussion about the conscience that occurred between Emanuel Hirsch (at this time, one of Tillich's Religious-Socialist colleagues) and Friedrich Gogarten. While conceding that Hirsch in his discussion with Gogarten had pressed his argument on behalf of the conscience in an unparadoxical and undialectical manner, the end result of which was a virtual absolutizing of the human conscience, Tillich in his turn is critical of Gogarten's assertion that "it is not the conscience but Christ, who is the place of revelation."[17] He makes his criticism, first, by denying any sort of absolute ground for the negative, dialectical critique that Gogarten leveled against Hirsch,[18]

16. *Ibid.*, 265.
17. *Ibid.*, 265.
18. Cf. *Systematic Theology*, I, 52.

and then, by defending the "autonomy" of the human spirit.

"Autonomy," as discussed and defended here by Tillich, is *not* self-will or arbitrariness;[19] it is obedience to the law of the self, obedience to the structure of human intellect and conscience. As such it is not in itself demonic; it does not represent the rebellion of man against God, as Gogarten would have it. It can *become* that, but in itself it is *not* that. If the autonomy of the human spirit were simply "fall and rebellion," Tillich argues, then Gogarten's own critique of Hirsch would share in that "fall and rebellion," since, according to Tillich, all the words and concepts that Gogarten uses are the creation of the autonomous human spirit.[20] What must be fought against is not autonomy as such, but the demonic and self-destroying misuse of autonomy. Like creation, the intellectual-spiritual life of man is reflective of the simultaneity of grace and judgment.

> There is no independent autonomy. It is always revelation and always hiddenness. There is always the divine and the demonic in autonomy. And the struggle of the divine and the demonic, the holy and the profane spirit, is the deepest, hidden content of man's intellectual-spiritual history

19. See Chapter IV below.
20. An oft-repeated argument by Tillich and one that he continued to press without seeming effect against Barth. Cf. Tillich, "What is Wrong with Dialectic Theology," *Journal of Religion*, XV. No. 2, (1935), p. 141–43. Cf. also *Systematic Theology*, I, 55,123,139f.; *Biblical Religion and the Search for Ultimate Reality*, (Chicago: Chicago University Press, 1955), pp. 7–10.

(*Geistesgeschichte*). It thus bears a seriousness
. . . and compels, in every moment and with
every thing, a choosing of sides, for the divine
or for the demonic.[21]

This struggle encompasses not only the conscience of
man, and the dialectical patterns of his reasoning, it
also takes in the spheres of the historical-critical sciences, the community, law, the state, and religion. Tillich takes pains to point out that religion by no means
possesses a monopoly on revelation or on the mani-
festation of grace and judgment. Revelation pervades
the realm of the profane as well as the religious. There
are, throughout culture, profane as well as religious
phenomena that make visible to the eyes of faith the
reality of grace and judgment. There are symbolically
powerful phenomena (*Erscheinungen*) in culture that,
though also standing under negation, make possible a
metaphysics of history, a symbolic, paradoxical, salvation history (*Heilsgeschichte*) embracing both culture
and religion. The perception of this dimension of life
affords a depth of meaning (*Tief-Sinn*, the equivalent
of the later "depth of reason") that comes to consciousness in faith's awareness of the ultimate unity of
life's "yes" and "no."[22]

After a brief excursus in which he turns back Gogarten's rejection of mystical experience and offers a
defense of an authentic awareness of the Unconditional, Tillich addresses himself to the final problem
set for discussion, the problem of history. He opens
this part of his discussion with the statement that it is

21. Tillich, "Kritisches und positives Paradox . . . ," 266.
22. *Ibid.*, 266–67.

46

a denial of the meaning of paradox to absolutize any historical reality, to admit, in such a form, an objectively manifest metaphysics of history. This basic principle, he says, has been perceived by Barth and Gogarten in their emphatic rejection of an empirical, supernatural as well as a liberal, humanistic conception of salvation-history. The Barth-Gogarten "critical paradox" makes impossible the equation of salvation-history with either profane-history or miracle-history (*Wundergeschichte*). Tillich however is critical of the fact that for Barth and Gogarten general history is marked essentially only by a negative sign. History is for them only the place of man's pretended God-likeness and, like nature and the human spirit, stands under the wrath of God.[23]

Against what he feels to be this unduly negative appraisal of general history, Tillich pursues a line of argument parallel to that used in the previous discussions of nature, and the human spirit, a line of argument that presupposes the logical necessity of the coincidence of opposites and that seeks to illumine the positive ground underlying every negative critique. In rejecting Barth and Gogarten's estimate of general history—or at least, his understanding of their views on the subject—Tillich points out that their assessment of "crisis" is possible only on the basis of a position that does not stand under this "judgment." Nowhere, Tillich asserts,

> are the positive roots of the negative paradox more manifest than here. For, the proclamation

23. *Ibid.*, 267.

of the crisis *is* history and its content is an historical content. Where this message is proclaimed, a place of revelation exists in the midst of history.[24]

But this "place of revelation," continues Tillich, cannot be understood as one small segment of history that is cut off from the rest and viewed as an object or thing. Rather, the revelation that takes place in history and that itself supports history is nonempirical (*unanschaulich*), that is, it is incapable of objectification in any direct way, though it is nonetheless real. This aspect of revelation Barth and Gogarten reject. They overlook, Tillich insists, the positive roots of their own "theology of crisis" and thus are forced to seek out a place in history on which to ground the proclamation of crisis. This place of revelation is Christ. It is thus in Christology that the conflict between the positive and the negative paradox is decisively expressed. The formulations of Gogarten, Tillich says,

> are especially instructive here. They mark off in history a once-for-all historical event, in which history is overcome and preserved (*aufgehoben*) and in which a New Thing is set. What happened in Christ happened beyond humanity (*jenseits des Menschentums*); but it happened in the historical man Jesus of Nazareth. It happened as simple, objective, historical fact. It happened once, and it happened once-for-all time. . . . Only

24. *Ibid.*, 267.

48

here does the "No" not apply to him to whom it appears.[25]

Commenting upon these formulations, Tillich charges that the "theology of the critical paradox," in seeking such a basis for its criticism, here becomes a "theology of the positively absurd." And with this step it has surrendered its own proper presupposition, the nonevidential, nonobjective character of faith. Faith is directed to a fixed point, to an objective historical fact. The acknowledgment of an empirical fact is taken up into the act of faith and through this breach unrestricted "heteronomy," "law," and "absolute religion" are introduced. A "heteronomy" is present that limits the critical-historical discipline in its quest for truth, that prevents its exploration of the possible nonoccurrence of the central fact, that hampers its questioning of "every act, every word, every gesture" of Jesus of Nazareth. A "law" is at hand that, having affirmed an absolute crisis of humanity, transforms every presupposition into an act of faith and thus establishes an intellectual asceticism no less restrictive than the practical asceticism of the mystics. Furthermore an "absolute religion" is established: a community is formed that claims for its own existence the same absoluteness over-against all other communities that it claims for the finite thing in which it believes.

This pattern of thought Tillich rejects. The nonempirical character (*Unanschaulichkeit*) of the revelation in Christ must be maintained: the empirical fact

25. *Ibid.*, 267–68.

points away from itself to the Unconditional that is nonobjectively manifested in it. Only in this manner are the dangers of heteronomy, law, and absolute religion to be avoided. Faith finally is not a work of affirming the absurd. It is a venturing-forth on the basis of a nonempirical revelation-history that pervades all history in a hidden way and that also finds full, symbolic expression in Christ. The community of believers that bears this faith is empirically indistinguishable and cuts across all the communities of cultural and religious history.[26]

Tillich concludes his criticism of the thought of Barth and Gogarten by asserting that the theology of crisis is quite right in its general fight against every presumptuous self-assertion of man in relation to the Unconditional and that this fight is no mere transitional phase of theology but represents a continuing and essential element in all theology. This struggle must, however, be based upon a presupposition which is itself no longer "crisis," no longer negative critique and judgment, but rather "creation" and "grace." This presupposition may be apprehended and spoken about only *through* "crisis," only paradoxically. It must be spoken of as being everywhere, in nature and in the human spirit, in culture and in religion. It can be spoken of in three ways: first, as the Eternal Source, the Ground, and the Abyss, that pervades all reality. It can be spoken of also as the Eternal Redemption, which is invisibly revealed to faith through the salvation history present in all history, and which is also present in a hidden, symbolically-powerful way in Christ. It can be spoken of as the Eternal Fulfillment,

26. *Ibid.*, 268.

the implicit Promise, in which the ambiguity of the Source and the struggle of the divine and the demonic is overcome and preserved in the eternal unity of God.

\* \* \*

It was in these terms that Tillich addressed his initial charges against Barth and Barth's theological friends. Barth responded to Tillich's criticism in a strongly polemical fashion. It is not necessary to recapitulate in detail all of Barth's reply. The major points, however, in that rebuttal and counterquestioning of Tillich are instructive and called forth a concluding statement by Tillich.

Barth was, he says, reluctant to reply in a public fashion to Tillich, especially since much of what Tillich had to say in his article was directed at Gogarten and only indirectly at himself. But, "having no grounds to ask to remain silent," he responded to the editor's request and joined in the "forced exchange of shots," as Barth describes it.[27]

As an opening point in his rebuttal of Tillich, Barth charges that Tillich's critique is not really a theological critique at all but is undertaken from the point of view of a philosophy of culture and as such is grounded on an entirely and characteristically non-theological presupposition. Barth does not directly identify what that presupposition is, but he insists that theology must be allowed to be theology and that one cannot criticize theology from some point outside. In response to Tillich's frequent warnings against "absolute religion" he raises a question about Tillich's un-

27. Karl Barth, "Von der Paradoxie des 'positiven Paradoxes,' Antworten und Fragen an Paul Tillich," *Theologische Blätter*, (Dec. 1923), II, 287.

derstanding of the kairos, inquiring how Tillich can be so sure that the times following World War I demand a rejection of absolutism and wondering if perhaps Gogarten's so-called "gesture of absolutism" is not also to be allowed the possibility of realization. Barth asks who finally *does* determine what the meaning of a given time is?

On another point he suggests that Tillich has not rightly understood the meaning of the term "crisis" as Barth has used it, that its meaning is not exclusively that of negation and prohibition, as Tillich seems to interpret it, but that it bears also the connotation of warning, admonition, and positive command (*Gebot*). Barth denies that his use of dialectical patterns of thought at any point gave rise to a quest for some theoretical ground on which to establish the dialectic itself, as if the dialectic were an end in itself. And he asks why it could not simply be a response to a real event.[28]

With regard to Tillich's own use of "dialectics," Barth expresses regret that Tillich has not taken pains to elaborate more fully what is meant by the phrase "positive paradox." It is not clear, Barth asserts, who the agent of the "real" transformation of critical negation into positive construct might be. If it is the intellectual achievement of the philosophical theologian, how can it be claimed, as Tillich does, that it derives from the Unconditional? If it is an act of God, how is it possible for man to recognize it as distinctly "other" in some nondialectical sense—that is, that it in fact derives from the Unconditional? In this context Barth

28. *Ibid.*, 289–90.

also asks about the meaning of "real": Does it stand in contrast to "ideal"? Are not the characteristics of the contingent and the unique (*das Einmalige*) indispensable to its definition? And what of the phrase "the Unconditional" (*das Unbedingte*)? Is "God" what is intended by this—in Barth's words—"frosty enormity?" Out of what philosophical tradition, Barth asks, does Tillich come to this "Unconditional" by which he is able to lay claim to nature, the human spirit, and history, and from which he is able to unfold not only a doctrine of science but also a doctrine of the Trinity? "I mean to understand," says Barth, "what is designated by this 'X' in which obviously we have to acknowledge the Tillichian 'positive paradox.' But I do not understand the stance (*Griff*)—so rebellious to me—by which, through a bold projection, Tillich makes himself master of the situation. . . . In earlier times one called it 'metaphysics.' "[29] Barth asks again:

> Is the positive paradox really the promised, supracritical (ground) . . . if its manifestation exists in the dogmatic establisment of a first principle—instead of in a question and answer, a seeking and finding, a falling and rising again; instead of in the representation of a history between the known and the knowing one, between man and God? The dogmatic establishment of this first principle makes the Church and the Holy Spirit, Scripture and Christ, superfluous. . . . With its unfolding everything, of itself, surrenders to the presupposition's most celebrated patterns, if one is only able

29. *Ibid.*, 291.

to think logically enough to find one's way in the manifold decrees of the "discoverer." It is this method, above all, which, with the first step into the temples of Tillich's thought, is strange and inconceivable to me and which, through its starting point, also makes its inferences as a whole so unbelievable as theology.[30]

Barth charges that if Tillich is really serious about the paradoxical character of the positive paradox, then he cannot be serious about the immediacy of the relationships he affirms between God and the world, nor the logical facility by which he thinks he is able to dispose of the positive and negative sides of these relationships, nor the liberality with which he believes he may distribute such relationships among the different "high and low dignitaries" of this age. Barth avers that one does not speak in such terms if one knows that as a theologian one has to do with the divine paradox— not simply with a nonempirical paradox (*das Unanschauliche*) but with One grounded simply in His own Will, who gives up His own Majesty and who, out of love and in love, is real and knowable in the world and by man. This God is known in a revelation that is not identical with a general "it is" and "there is" relationship easily discoverable by man. He is known in a special revelation initiated from God's side, a revelation in which men are known by Him in person-to-person encounter. It is here, Barth says, that Tillich's theological course and his own markedly diverge.[31]

This point is borne out in Christology. Barth asserts,

30. *Ibid.*, 291.
31. *Ibid.*, 292–93.

54

"For 'us' Christ is salvation-history, salvation-history itself, Christ is the 'positive paradox'; for Tillich, Christ is the representation, in perfect symbol-power (*Symbol-Kraft*), of a more or less always and over-all occurring salvation-history."[32] Barth rejects Tillich's assertion that the limitation of revelation to a fixed place in history, to a segment of history, destroys the nonobjective character of faith, and he makes the counterassertion that this charge by Tillich shows how Tillich's own incomplete definition of the paradoxical character of the positive paradox catches him short: intent upon the very serious mark of the nonempirical, he loses sight of the divine freedom and love. Barth then charges that Tillich runs the most serious danger of transforming the justified polemic against a man-made god into its opposite, the polemic against the Incarnation. The "positive paradox," for Barth, bears not only the quality of the nonempirical; it is above all God's special, personal, "real" (inclusive of particularity and contingency) act of freedom and love. One says it is nonempirical because it is an act of *God's* freedom and love, but it also occurred "once upon a time" because it was an act of God's *freedom* and *love*. The "positive paradox," through the apostolic witness, is bound up inextricably with an empirical fact from which it cannot be abstracted. It is the revelation of Majesty in the lowliness of an empirical, "at that time," "misunderstandable" fact, and only as such is it the "positive paradox." "Thus Christian talk about Christ and all Christology remains necessarily dialectical. In order to guard the 'positive paradox,' it must

32. *Ibid.*, 293. Fr. Tavard makes this same point in his criticism of Tillich's Christology. Cf. *Op. cit.*, pp. 103, 172–73.

continually reckon with the possibility of scandal, a possibility implicit in the historical element in the apostolic witness."[33] Such Christian talk about Christ may never mistake itself for its object. It ought not sabotage the positive paradox given in the historical witness to Christ by distinguishing, with the help of symbol theory, between an "eternal salvation" and "Jesus of Nazareth."

Barth concludes his counter-critique by saying that he is not at all in sympathy with a theology that indulges the free spirit of Protestant self-will and invention, even when that happens "under the banner of 'Theonomy.'" Not only God, not only Christianity, but also the Church to which one individually belongs is the presupposition of theology. One cannot eliminate the "positive paradox" in this form any more than one can do so with the scandalous historicity and factuality of revelation. It is not the standpoint of faith that is at issue. Nor is it Gogarten's view of revelation or the "theology of crisis." It is rather, according to Barth, the affirmation of the indissoluable correlation of the theological concept of truth with the concepts of Church, Canon, and Holy Spirit. He ends his summation with a quotation from Augustine: *"In ecclesia non valet: hoc ego dico, hoc tu dicis, hoc ille dicit, sed: haec dicit Dominus."*[34]

Such represents the major points—certainly not the whole—of Barth's reply to Tillich. He concludes his remarks by acknowledging that although, on the

33. *Ibid.,* 294.
34. "In the church it is not valid [to say]: I say this, you say this, he says this; but rather the Lord says these things." *Ibid.,* 296.

whole, Tillich had initiated the discussion in a manner friendly and appreciative of the so-called "theology of crisis," he, Barth, finds himself unable to reply in kind. He is unable to do so, he says, because the corrective that Tillich seeks to bring to bear on the "theology of crisis" is in fact an attack upon the decisive point that Barth had been trying to make. He further asserts that what Tillich proposes is something that has had its own strong appeal to himself. This fact has its part to play in his "somewhat spirited" response to Tillich's views.

In the same December (1923) issue of *Theologische Blätter*, which contained Barth's reply to Tillich's initial critique, Tillich published a brief and moderate answer to Barth. He in no way attempted to answer each of Barth's many countercharges and questions;[35] and he carefully sought to avoid what he termed "small defensive impulses against ironically or pedagogically superior formulations."[36] Rather he chose to restate in simple terms his own understanding of the kairos and what he felt this should mean for the responsible theologian.

He begins by frankly admitting that there is a very close connection between his philosophical-theological work, his positive and negative criticism of Barth and Gogarten, and the contemporary historical situation

35. Barth in his correspondence with Thurneysen expressed disappointment at Tillich's failure to answer directly many of the questions he had put to him. Cf. James D. Smart (trans.), *Revolutionary Theology in the Making: Barth-Thurneysen Correspondence, 1914–1925*, (Richmond, Va.: John Knox Press, 1964) p. 160.

36. Paul Tillich, "Antwort"; *Theologische Blätter*, (Dec. 1923), II, 296.

and all that it reveals of man's spiritual condition. It is in the context of the contemporary intellectual-spiritual situation (*Geisteslage*) that his own thought is to be understood. The concept of the kairos means for Tillich "that one cannot say and do everything in every time, but that every time has the task to create anew out of its own life and in its own words the eternal meaning of all time."[37] With this reassertion of the kairos concept, Tillich then proceeds to spell out what this means for the present moment.

He agrees with Barth's judgment that Tillich's own struggle against the "Grand Inquisitor" is essentially a struggle against "heteronomy" and "the Law." Tillich insists, however, that this struggle must be pressed further than it has been in the past. It must move beyond the false alternative of "loss of salvation" or "destruction of truthfulness" that characterized Orthodoxy and Pietism—and even liberal theology. It must affirm the fact that salvation does not come by good works, not even a good work of belief that views a certain content of faith as the condition of salvation and then calls that content "God" or "Christ" or "Jesus." It must recognize that there is a "justification" of the "unreligious," of "atheists," and of "blasphemers of the Son of Man," if only the spirit of truth is not blasphemed. The purity of faith must be guarded against every form of intellectual works-righteousness that may arise out of orthodoxy, liberalism, or even out of the new critical-dialectical patterns of thought that seek to proclaim the Paradox.[38]

37. *Ibid.*, 296.
38. *Ibid.*, 296–97.

This, Tillich says, is one side of the current intellectual-spiritual situation against which his thought must be understood. But there is a second aspect of the present situation that must be considered: Barth says the Canon, Church, and Holy Spirit are the presuppositions of theology and its concept of truth. This may be true as a general statement but what does it mean, Tillich asks, for the present spiritual situation? Here Tillich asserts that it is fruitless and meaningless to try to use the old words in the old ways. They simply no longer express their real essence. This is the work and the guilt of the "Grand Inquisitor," the law, heteronomy, and objectification. It is under this fate that everyone at present stands, theologians and nontheologians alike. Tillich insists that it is impossible for those who are aware of the present situation to speak of God as if this word could mediate directly the power originally associated with it. "Therefore one must speak of the 'Unconditional.' It is not as though this were a substitute concept, but rather it is a key to be used to open the closed door to the Holy of Holies of the name 'God' and to other things and then to be thrown away."[39]

In like manner Tillich argues that it is wrong to speak directly or immediately of Jesus Christ as the positive paradox as is done in Gogarten's discussion of revelation. It is not to avoid a genuine "offense" or "scandal" that something else must be said at this point; it is rather to avoid making the one who acts (i.e., God) the guilty party instead of man. Even the

39. *Ibid.*, 297.

name of Jesus Christ can be used in making a false scandal.

> If the Spirit of Christ were one with the name Jesus Christ, so would the blasphemer of the name be damned and the Grand Inquisitor be right. But the Spirit of Christ, the Positive Paradox, does not exhaust itself in the empirical appearance. Even theology has never asserted the absolute contingency of the Positive Paradox. It has rather spoken of the Logos which, in Jewish and heathen history, leads thither revealingly to the complete revelation. Theology may not be barred from following this way and making visible what is presently becoming manifest among 'heathen and Jews,' that is, in the creation and crises of autonomous culture.[40]

Tillich denies that one "bows down before false altars" by proclaiming the Positive Paradox in terms that identify the creations and ruins of culture as the invisible-visible marks of the divine "Yes" and "No." Perhaps, Tillich says, it is because one does not refer to these things in the words of Scripture and Church that one may call this "culture-philosophy." But

> the present situation forces one as a theologian to be *not* a theologian but a philosopher of culture. If one prefers not to call the spirit which is effective in all this the "Holy Spirit," then theology, for the sake of the spirit of truth and love,

40. *Ibid.*, 297.

60

waits for the Holy Spirit; or better, it must declare that the Holy Spirit blows where it will, and that the Spirit of Christ, the spirit of the concrete Paradox, can blow upon us stronger out of the splendor and the death of the flowers of the field, out of the creative power and the despair of a work of art, out of the depth of meaning and the self-annulment of a logic, . . . than it can out of words, stories, and pictures which bear for our consciousness always the image of the Grand Inquisitor.[41]

It is in the light of this spiritual situation that Tillich says his thought must be viewed. And it is this spiritual situation, he argues, that the theologian must take upon himself if he is not to become unfaithful. For it is possible also for one to be unfaithful to his times through "a disparagement of culture and the abandonment of oneself to absolute contingency."[42] To do this is to destroy the bond of fellowship with those who in all areas of cultural life struggle for the revelation of the positive paradox and the realization of the spirit of Christ. At times one must decide *for* the spirit of truth and love and *against* a "holy" spirit that is bound to the empty, if concrete, forms of "Canon" and "Church."

With this restatement of his understanding of the kairos in its immediacy, Tillich then addressed two brief, final words to Barth. In the first he expressed a fear that the particular manner in which Barth and Gogarten make use of dialectics may lead past the dia-

41. *Ibid.*, 298.
42. *Ibid.*

lectical position itself into a very positive but very un-dialectical supernaturalism. He is apprehensive that out of the "Yes" and "No" of the relationship of God to the world—which is essential to every dialectic—a simple "no" over-against the world will be defined and that this will be followed in turn by a positive, undia-lectical "Yes" that will destroy the creative tension between God and the world. If this happens, Tillich warns, cultural stagnation will inevitably ensue.

The second word that Tillich addressed to Barth is in a way related to this first word. He sees Barth as persisting in a Calvinistic inclination toward dualism, the dualism of the profane and the sacred. The end result of such an attitude, Tillich asserts, is a profana-tion and deprivation of cultural life on the one hand and a primitivizing of religious life on the other. Til-lich asserts that he, for one, cannot count it a gain, in the present situation, to have the profanation of culture defined as unalterable. In opposition to this attitude Tillich sets himself "in the German Lutheran tradition, the historical-spiritual significance of which exists in the fact that ever new attempts have been initiated to overcome a profane autonomy through a theonomous autonomy. Schleiermacher and Hegel stand in this line."[43] Though Tillich makes clear that he dissociates himself at points from Schleiermacher and Hegel, he "enthusiastically" joins them in their concern to make visible in the common forms of logic and ethics a ref-erence to the Paradox, thereby transforming profane autonomy into theonomy. With this concluding word

43. *Ibid.*, 298–99. It is a little difficult, I think, to follow Tillich in his historical-cultural analysis at this point—both in regard to Calvinism and German Lutheranism.

Tillich ended his statement of disagreement with Barth.

*     *     *

The discussion, in one sense, ended here. In another sense, it continued through the years, for neither man essentially abandoned the positions defined in this early exchange of views. It is clear that Tillich was arguing, over-against Barth, for a principle of immanent dynamism—not, of course, devoid of transcendent dimensions, but the orientation was consistently this-worldly. Contributing to this purpose was Tillich's refusal to objectify and personify the Unconditional, or to represent the Unconditional as standing over-against the world. Rather he conceived of the Unconditional as the ultimate source of both the "Yes" and the "No" in history's continuing course of creation and ruin, grace and judgment. Barth, on the other hand, affirmed God as transcendent and dynamic, a personal being who exists independent of creation and who, in his freedom, uniquely reveals himself in the historical event of Christ, and who, again in his freedom, continues to reveal himself through the once-for-all-time character of that event and the Scriptural witness to it.

One must underline the fact that although this exchange of views with Barth in 1923 does not provide a picture of all the ideational factors in Tillich's philosophical position, it does reflect a continuity of concern—on Tillich's part—that carries back before World War I to Tillich's student days. One need not attach major significance to the controversy in its effect upon the course of Tillich's own intellectual development. It is likely that some personal animosity

63

was engendered by the sharpness of some of the criticisms and rejoinders, and that this may have had a tendency to fix each man more firmly in his own patterns of thought. It is clear that further dialogue did not follow. Barth, for example, does not make extensive reference to the work of Tillich in his later multivolume *Church Dogmatics*. Tillich by contrast *does* make more frequent reference to Barth in his writings. He obviously continued to regard Barth's thought as a major antithetical point of view.[44] But the substance of his criticism of Barth did not significantly change over the years. That there was a shifting of position in Tillich's later thought can and must be noted—but this seems to have come about more as a result of a crisis within Religious Socialism itself than from criticisms directed at Tillich by Barth and those sympathetic with Barth's position. It is to this crisis within Religious Socialism then that we next turn in giving account of Tillich's continuing effort to provide systematic and existential viability for his projected alternative to traditional interpretations of Christian faith and life.

44. Cf. *Systematic Theology*, 6–8, p. 41, p. 139, etc. It should perhaps be noted that in later years both Barth and Tillich exchanged friendly visits. Before his retirement from Basel in 1962 Barth began holding occasional seminars devoted to a study of Tillich's *Systematic Theology*.

# III

## The Hirsch Affair—and After

In the year following the discussion with Barth, Tillich, at the friendly urging of the German minister of education, accepted a theological professorship at the University of Marburg. He seems not to have been enthusiastic about the change. He speaks of having made the shift against his own real desire.[1] There, at Marburg, in 1924–25, he met "the first radical effects of the neo-orthodox theology."[2] This was manifested among students in a general disregard for the major philosophical-historical problems associated with the question of the relationship of religion and culture. Such an attitude clearly ran counter to Tillich's own focus of interest.

This situation may have occasioned, as Tillich as-

1. Kegley and Bretall, p. 14.
2. *Ibid.*, p. 14.

serts,[3] the commencement of work on the *Systematic Theology*, but it certainly does not represent a significant turning point in Tillich's own thought. An analysis of his writings during the years 1924–25 yields no evidence of any alteration of concern or any major change in emphasis. What these years—and the years that followed—seemed to represent more than anything else was a maturing of Tillich's earlier thought in the context of critical converse. One can cite, for example, the 1924 lecture at Giessen on the theme of "Justification and Doubt,"[4] an obvious elaboration of an earlier idea now set forth in relation to contemporary, alternative schools of thought. Also, in 1925, Tillich published the very important "Philosophy of Religion,"[5] drawing together in systematic form many of the major philosophical concepts implicit in his earlier thought. In fact, were it not for the identification of his classroom lectures at Marburg with "the beginning of my work on this system,"[6] one could with good reason suggest that this 1925 treatise itself was the beginning of the later three volumes of *Systematic Theology*. It bears many parallels with the later system.

The stay at Marburg was brief, extending over only three semesters. In the fall of 1925 Tillich left Marburg to become Professor of the Science of Religion at the University of Dresden. In making this change

3. *Ibid.*, p. 14. See above, pp. 16–18.
4. "Rechtfertigung und Zweifel," *Vorträge der theologischen Konferenz zu Giessen*. (Giessen: Topelmann, 1924).
5. "Religionsphilosophie," in *Lehrbuch der Philosophie*, edited by Max Dessoir, (Berlin: Ullstein, 1925).
6. *Systematic Theology*, III, 7.

he turned down "a more traditional theological position" at Giessen, in part at least, because of the cultural appeal of Dresden and the "openness of the big city."[7] Again, his writings during the years at Dresden reflect a continuation of previous concerns. In 1926 he published his thought-provoking analysis of the contemporary historical situation, *The Religious Situation of the Present*[8] (translated into English in 1932 as *The Religious Situation*). In this work Tillich seems to have recognized a weakness in the Religious-Socialist movement. He admits that it lacked the historical force necessary to transform the German political situation.[9] But throughout the book he strongly affirmed the movement's underlying principles, especially the kairos concept.

In the same year, 1926, Tillich offered further explication of the kairos concept in two essays in a two-volume work, *Kairos*, which he himself edited.[10] In the second of the two essays, "Kairos and Logos," Tillich attempted to reconcile the stabilities of truth with the realities of a changing historical situation and thus carry forward the development of his philosophy of history (his "metaphysics of history" as he refers to it in *The Religious Situation*). In 1926 he also delivered and published a lecture on the subject of "The Demonic" (*Das Dämonische*), the creative but ultimately

7. Kegley and Bretall, p. 14. While at Dresden Tillich also served as a professor of theology at the University of Leipzig.
8. *Die religiöse Lage der Gegenwart*, (Berlin: Ullstein, 1926).
9. *The Religious Situation*, (New York: Meridian Books, Inc., 1956), pp. 175–77, 211, 218–19.
10. *Kairos :I: Zur Geisteslage und Geisteswendung*, (Darmstadt: Reichl, 1926).

self-destructive principle present in every kairos situation. These patterns of thought, apparent throughout his stay at the University of Dresden, persisted also through the course of his appointment as professor of philosophy at the University of Frankfurt, a position assumed in 1929. Of his academic career from World War I down to 1933 Tillich observed: "A constant change of faculties and yet no change in subject."[11] There is certainly no reason to question this assessment.

With his move to Frankfurt in 1929, however, important changes *did* occur in the external conditions of his life. In the succeeding years he became increasingly involved in the struggle against Hitler and National Socialism. At many points Tillich stood opposed to the authoritarian ideology of the Nazi movement, and he spoke out publicly against it. In 1932, for example, he testified against a group of Nazi thugs responsible for a riot within the grounds of the University.[12] Such opposition was not forgotten and when Hitler came to power in 1933, Tillich was among the first professors to be dismissed from university positions. It was this event that brought Tillich's academic career in Germany to an end and that led to his emigration to America. Reinhold Niebuhr, who had been impressed by some of Tillich's writings—his brother H. Richard Niebuhr had translated *Die religiöse Lage der Gegenwart* into English in 1932—was visiting in Germany during the summer of 1933 and, upon hearing of Tillich's removal from the professorship at Frankfurt, urged Tillich to accept a position at Union

11. *Interpretation of History*, p. 40.
12. *Time*, (March 16, 1959), LXXXIII, 48.

Theological Seminary in New York City. Tillich accepted, and on November 4, 1933, he, with his wife and two children, arrived in New York to take up life in a challenging, new environment.

Not long after assuming his new position in America, Tillich made public a significant break in relationships with one of his close colleagues and friends in the Religious-Socialist movement, Emanuel Hirsch. For want of a better term the incident will be referred to simply as "the Hirsch affair." It is an important incident not only for the light it sheds upon Tillich's views "in crisis" but also because it helps to illumine further some of the peculiar intricacies and problems of the kairos doctrine. Furthermore, it provides major aid in identifying what can be considered the one major shift in the over-all development of Tillich's thought.

\*  \*  \*

Emanuel Hirsch, a theologian and sometime Biblical scholar, was an early participant in the German Religious-Socialist movement. Although Tillich did not always agree with some of Hirsch's philosophical and theological views,[13] he generally found in Hirsch a strong supporter of his own attempts to provide a statement of Christian faith expressly oriented towards the contemporary historical-cultural situation. Throughout the 1920's Hirsch proved to be an influential proponent of the views of Religious Socialism. With Hitler's rise to power in 1933, however, Hirsch suddenly severed his ties with Religious Socialism and spoke out in support of the "New Germany." He soon became a

13. See above, p. 44. Cf. also "Rechtfertigung und Zweifel," *op. cit.*, p. 26.

leading figure among the government-supported "German Christians," a party within the Evangelical Church that sought to align church policy and structure with the program of the national government. Hirsch, along with most German Christians, endorsed the idea that in the natural orders of race, folk, and nation there existed a revelation of God of equal value with, if not superior to, that of Scripture.

Within the churches bitter theological and political debate broke out. Lines of battle were drawn; old friendships were broken. Karl Barth became a leader in the opposition to Nazi attempts to infiltrate and manipulate the churches. His old friend and supporter, Friedrich Gogarten, however, joined forces with the German Christians.[14] During the course of the summer of 1933 Barth issued a forceful attack against the program of the German Christians in a pamphlet, "Theological Existence Today." Barth's attack called forth an answer from Hirsch, also in pamphlet form, "What the German Christians Want for the Church." Then, in the following year, 1934, Hirsch followed up the first reply to Barth with a detailed, systematic statement of his German Christian position. In this later work, *The Present Intellectual Situation in the Light of Philosophical and Theological Reflection*,[15] Hirsch

14. In a letter in the final issue of the theological periodical, *Zwischen den Zeiten* (No. 6, 1933), Barth rejected the attempt by Gogarten to ground Christian theology on an existential understanding of man. He strongly opposed Gogarten's effort to equate the law of God with the "law of the German folk" (pp. 537–39).

15. *Die gegenwärtige geistige Lage in Spiegel philosophischer und theologischer Besinnung.* (Gottingen: Vandenhoeck and Ruprecht, 1934). For Barth's reaction to Hirsch's

made use of many of the concepts of Religious Socialism, especially the kairos idea. He avoided direct use
of the term, however, and failed generally to make
clear his conceptual dependence upon Religious
Socialism.

Tillich apparently did not play a leading role in the
controversies within the church during the summer of
1933. Later, however, from New York, he felt impelled to offer a public reply to Hirsch's philosophical
statement of support for National Socialism. Thus, on
October 1, 1934, he sent back to Germany a lengthy
"open letter" to Hirsch, which was published in the
November issue of *Theologische Blätter*. The open
letter was entitled "The Theology of the Kairos and
the Present Intellectual Situation". Although the arguments in the letter are somewhat involved and at points
quite repetitious, the letter offers valuable insight into
aspects of Tillich's thought. In it Tillich takes pains to
identify the philosophical-theological origins not only
of Hirsch's thought but also, in part, of his own. He
underlines the theological differences between Hirsch
and himself and discusses some of the more difficult
theoretical problems with which he had wrestled over
the years. The letter deserves closer scrutiny than it
has generally received from interpreters of Tillich's
thought.

\*　　\*　　\*

In the introduction of the open letter, Tillich begins with an explanation of the form of communication. He asserts that the content of his letter has both

book, see Karl Barth, *The German Church Conflict* "Ecu-
menical Studies in History," (Richmond: John Knox Press,
1965), pp. 30–33.

personal and public import and that it comes as a response to the publication of Hirsch's book. He confesses astonishment at Hirsch's use of many of the basic concepts of Religious Socialism in the cause of National Socialism and expresses concern that these concepts have not been identified as arising out of the Religious-Socialist movement. He further charges that the manner in which Hirsch makes use of these ideas robs them of their deepest meaning.[16]

As an addendum to this opening assault Tillich insists that the "demands of the political struggle" should not be allowed to override the discipline of truthful, critical analysis; he suggests that Hirsch, in the course of his book, has failed to display an independence of the critical, scholarly function from the present political situation. In this connection he professes disappointment that Hirsch should make use of the term "Religious Marxism" in his references to the Religious-Socialist movement. Tillich avers that this practice by Hirsch is an obvious attempt to discredit Religious Socialism through appeal to popular, anti-Marxist prejudice. This is especially difficult to understand, Tillich asserts, in view of the fact that Hirsch himself is profoundly in the debt of Religious Socialism for many of his most important interpretations and concepts. That Hirsch should suddenly have seen fit to deny the effective agency of the German working class in the struggle for a new future, that he should now affirm "the revolutionary powers of the middle-class and conservative groups"—this is conceivable to

16. "Die Theologie des Kairos und die gegenwärtige geistige Lage," *Theologische Blätter*, XXIII, No. 11 (November 1934) 305–6.

Tillich.[17] But that he should attempt to disown and conceal his common theoretical ties with Religious Socialism, this Tillich finds incomprehensible and unacceptable. Therefore, to avoid any misunderstanding by others, Tillich sets about to trace in detail the origins of Hirsch's ideas and outline the points of variance with his own thought.

Recalling his own earlier description of the "religious situation,"[18] Tillich remarks that at the time of publication of that work, he had sent Hirsch a copy of the book and had received in reply a question from Hirsch as to why Tillich had cast himself in the role of a spectator, that is, as one who *describes* a situation rather than one who changes it. In answer to that question Tillich had argued that without some basic orientation to the past, the present, and the future it was imposible to fulfill the demand of thinking "out of the hour." He then notes that Hirsch in his present work has come around fully to Tillich's earlier view, that Hirsch now offers his own appraisal of "the present spiritual situation," making extensive use of historical analyses as a means of defining the needs of the hour and the hopes for the future. Beyond this point of formal identity, however, Tillich charges that much of Hirsch's historical analysis parallels the Religious-Socialist understanding of history. The description of the theonomous culture of the Middle Ages, the account of its destruction through the rise of "autonomous reason," the catastrophe of the "world-shaping will" of rationalism in World War I, the characterization of the present day as a struggle for new cultural

17. *Ibid.*, 307.
18. *Die religiöse Lage der Gegenwart.*

substance: all of these ideas have their counterpart in Religious-Socialist theory. And Tillich asks Hirsch why he does not make these lines of dependence clear.

Actually the list of points of similarity between Hirsch's interpretation of history and Tillich's is much longer, and Tillich does not neglect to cite the whole of it. But much more important and basic is Tillich's discussion of Hirsch's use of the kairos concept. He notes that although Hirsch shuns actual use of the Greek word the ideas associated with that word are everywhere apparent in Hirsch's book. Hirsch, for example, speaks repeatedly of "the present hour" and "the awakening," of the "special responsibility which the present hour holds for theology and philosophy," of "the religious meaning of our historical moment," of "openness for the demand of this hour of history."[19] All these words and phrases, Tillich claims, are derivatives of the kairos concept. More than that they are really only substitutes for it. Addressing himself to Hirsch, Tillich writes:

> From [your] adoption of the kairos idea follow points of fundamental agreement in philosophy and theology. You are striving for an existential philosophy of history—for what I in my last German lecture attempted to develop as "existential-historical method." A sentence [from your book] such as: "the existence of the one who philosophizes becomes the measure of the historical, existential quality of philosophy" is an almost word for word rendition of a basic idea out of

19. "Die Theologie des Kairos . . . ," 306.

74

[my] *Gläubiger Realismus* ["Belief-ful Realism"] . . . [Your] "self-elucidation of the new German reality in conformity with its existential depths" was the endeavor of Religious Socialism from first to last. None of our writings had basically any other content. We [also] attempted, as you [now] demand, "to allow the hour to become powerful in us . . . in order not to fail our task."[20]

After identifying points of contact in the kairos idea Tillich proceeds to question Hirsch on his use of this doctrine in the German Christian cause. He asks Hirsch if he realizes that his demand for existential-historical thought runs counter to the theoretical position of his new-found ally, Gogarten. He declares that Hirsch and Gogarten can join forces in the present situation only on the basis of self-deception and expresses doubt that Gogarten, who once described Tillich's kairos doctrine as a "pestilence," will now, for political reasons, accept Hirsch's "species of the same thing with more grace."[21]

Tillich's questioning of Hirsch moves deeper still. He asks Hirsch whether he is aware of the fact that in his call for existential-historical thought he has joined himself philosophically with the one man "of all the living and dead" with whom he would least wish to be associated, i.e., Karl Marx. In a few very illuminating sentences Tillich observes:

Whereas the understanding of existence with Kierkegaard, to whom you make appeal, and with

20. *Ibid.*, 309.
21. *Ibid.*, 309.

Heidegger, of whom you disapprove, and with Jaspers, whom you do not mention, is arrived at by way of the existence of the individual, the young Marx . . . demanded, over-against Hegel and even more so over-against Feuerbach, existential-historical thought. Religious Socialism, which in this respect really was Religious Marxism, received this as its *only* demand and, consistent with its powers, implemented this demand. When you call for existential-historical thought you are dependent upon the young Marx. . . . And you and we and Marx and everyone who thinks in this manner is dependent upon ancient Jewish prophecy. . . .[22]

Tillich thus sets Hirsch in the tradition of Marx and "Jewish prophecy"—observations that were undoubtedly intended to embarrass Hirsch but that at the same time illumine the philosophical linage of the kairos concept.

Further elucidation of this central concept comes when Tillich describes the philosophical implications and problems connected with its formulation. At one point in his book Hirsch argued for a dynamic concept of truth. Tillich takes up this "suggestion" by Hirsch and identifies it as the major philosophical objective of his own previous labors. He asks:

Without here going into your formulations, might I remind you that the problem which you pose with them was the theme of all the work

22. *Ibid.*, 309.

devoted to the philosophical grounding of the kairos doctrine, that the solutions have had effect far beyond our circle, that since that time we have spoken of a "dynamic truth" and have attempted to develop a "dynamic method"?"[23]

Tillich proceeds to point out that it was out of this context that the concept of the "risk-character" of knowledge arose, that elaboration of this idea is to be found in Tillich's discussion of knowledge as "fate" and "risk" in the essay "Kairos und Logos." Tillich explains that it was in connection with the idea of "dynamic truth" that the communal character of knowledge was explored in an effort to avoid individual caprice and arbitrariness. Knowledge was viewed as arising "out of" and happening "for" a community. To this idea the Religious-Socialist movement itself bore witness in its attempt to seek out the locus of greatest historical vitality and power among the people and, through association with the working class, to illumine the historical existence both of the German people and culture in general.[24]

Tillich in summarizing this phase of his discussion states that he would not have been forced to this sort of documentation of Hirsch's ties with Religious Socialism—and of course with his own thought—if Hirsch had not attempted to veil and obscure this relationship. He observes: "The older generation knows

23. *Ibid.*, 310.
24. For a further statement on the source of this idea, see "Existential Philosophy: Its Historical Meaning" in *Theology of Culture*, (New York: Oxford University Press, 1959), p. 89. Cf. also Tillich's very important discussion, "Masse und Geist," *Gesammelte Werke*, II, 35–90.

77

of these things and shakes its head." And he then asks Hirsch: "But how can you answer to the younger generation, which knows nothing . . . of all this, for the fact that you give them a picture of the development [of your thought] which shuts off from them an understanding of the real development?"[25]

From this description of the origins of Hirsch's thought and his use of the kairos idea, Tillich turns to an analysis of the aspect of the kairos doctrine that was excised by Hirsch in order to adapt it for use in the Nazi cause. He recalls for Hirsch the important distinction which had been made between the idea of the "sacramental" and the "prophetic," between the consecration of a historical actuality and an awareness of the Holy come "close at hand" as in Jesus' preaching of the "kingdom of God." The latter, the prophetic point of view, is bearer both of promise and demand. It is eschatological in character. Tillich observes:

> This eschatological moment is inseparable from the kairos doctrine as found in early Christianity and also in Religious Socialism. It binds us to Barth, in so far as we with him deny the palpable presence of the Divine in a finite being or event; it separates us from Barth, because the eschatological has with him a supranatural character whereas with us it has a paradoxical character. We do not place the Transcendent in an undialectical antithesis to the historical, but believe that it can only be understood as genuine transcend-

25. "Die Theologie des Kairos . . . ," col. 311.

ence when it is understood as that which now and
again breaks into history, shakes it, and turns it.
In this conception you and we stand together.
The theory of the kairos stands exactly in the
middle between the theology of the recent national Lutheranism and the dialectical theology.
It views the second as a deviation into abstract
transcendence, the first as a deviation into demonic sacramentalism.[26]

Tillich seems once more to set himself with Hirsch
against Barth, but this is only momentary, for he goes
on immediately to assert that over-against both abstract transcendence and demonic sacramentalism the
"prophetic, early Christian paradox" understands the
kingdom of God as both entering into history and
*yet always remaining above history*. Such an understanding of the Kingdom of God, Tillich asserts, does

26. *Ibid.*, 312. This quotation suggests that if there was
some influence of Barth upon Tillich the most likely area of
such influence was in the realm of eschatology. Barth's 1919
work *Der Römerbrief (The Epistle to the Romans)* is radically eschatological in tone. By contrast Tillich's 1919 lecture
"Ueber die Idee einer Theologie der Kultur" ("Concerning
the Idea of a Theology of Culture") is much less so, and
his subsequent writings seem to reflect a heightening of the
eschatological note. It should be observed, however, that
there are independent roots for Tillich's eschatology in his
definition of God as the Unconditional, the Ground of the
subject-object cleavage, and in Schelling's strong condemnation of "pharisaism." In fact, Tillich himself testifies to an
independent origin of his eschatological viewpoint; cf. "Die
Überwindung des Religionsbegriff in der Religionsphilosophie," *Gesammelte Werke*, I, pp 367–68. Any dogmatic as-
sertions about Barth's influence upon Tillich seem ill-advised.
See above, p. 39 n. 7.

not lend itself to "the undialectical necessities of the political-ecclesiastical struggle." And he then expresses the hope that there may be theologians and non-theologians on both sides of the current church conflict who will find in the undistorted kairos doctrine a way out of the blind alleys into which both Hirsch and Barth are separately bound to lead theology and the church. Tillich states forthrightly, however, that if sides must be chosen in the present situation he chooses that side which defends eschatology against the attack of a demonic sacramentalism. Of this choice he says: "Even if a high price must be paid for this in the form of supranatural contraction and orthodox rigidity, it is better than the sacrifice of the eschaton to an absolutized finite reality."[27] Then, as a summary of Hirsch's error, he baldly declares: "You pervert the prophetic, eschatologically-conceived kairos doctrine into a priestly-sacramental consecration of a present historical event."[28]

With this declaration Tillich makes clear his major philosophical-theological difference with Hirsch. He does not, however, allow the case to rest simply with a statement of the charge. He goes on to show what the effect of Hirsch's neglect of eschatology and prophetism has upon his understanding of both the past and present. Tillich points out that whereas Religious Socialism had always guarded itself against enthusiastic claims in the struggle to realize a more vital society, this restraint is now absent in the work of Hirsch. Hirsch, he charges, has yielded to the temptation of making absolute historical evaluations. Thus, the year

27. *Ibid.*, 312.
28. *Ibid.*

80

1918, the year of the defeat of Germany in World War I, is described in completely negative terms whereas the year 1933, the year of Hitler's rise to power, is viewed in an uncritically positive fashion. These sorts of evaluations, Tillich claims, are without theological justification and can be made "only on the basis of a certainty that one is himself living in the age of perfect grace."[29] Such, Tillich declares, is an absurdity. The year 1933 cannot be placed on the same level as the year 33 in the history of salvation. Hirsch, Tillich suggests, would do better to follow the example of Religious Socialism, avoid the black and white categorization of years and epochs, and seek to appraise soberly the vital and effective forces operative in every epoch and in every situation. Tillich avers that it was because Religious Socialism was able to preserve the prophetic, eschatological perspective that its social-political analyses proved as effective and meaningful as they were. It was this which underlay the "belief-ful realism" of Religious Socialism, a realism that has now given way in Hirsch to "unrestrained enthusiasm."

With these comments and observations Tillich was, of course, criticizing the absence of a critical, "protestant" spirit in Hirsch's statement of the kairos doctrine. Tillich, as a matter of fact, presses this charge of a lack of critical thinking in several specific areas of Hirsch's thought. But these additional critiques, with two exceptions, add little to an understanding of Tillich's own thought. In the case of the two exceptions observations *are* made that cast light upon aspects of his thought and deserve mention.

29. *Ibid.*, 313.

In the first instance Tillich is at pains to identify and reject Hirsch's utopianism, a point already made in substance. Here, however, he reminds Hirsch that, in the course of supporting the general socialist movement, Religious Socialism never abandoned its critical function. From first to last, Tillich argues, Religious Socialism fought against utopian features of socialist theory and warned of the inevitable disillusionment and despair that would result from such an ideological emphasis. As an absolutizing of a finite possibility, Tillich insists that utopianism must be firmly rejected. In making this point Tillich recalls an early stage in the development of Religious-Socialist theory:

> . . . we did not want to destroy the burden of the demand and the passion of the expectation. In this need—I can remember exactly the day— the kairos idea was discovered. It was discovered —as perhaps many do not know—in the struggle with the problem of utopia. Thereby a position was provided from which we had the possibility of appreciating the significance of the historical moment for the structuring of the future without becoming utopians.[30]

In concluding his criticism of Hirsch's utopianism, Tillich warns that Hirsch must share responsibility for the crisis of despair that lies ahead for the German people if the visionary preachments of National Socialism go unchecked.

At a second point in his indictment of Hirsch's

30. *Ibid.*, 314.

failure to exercise a critical function, Tillich makes some brief comments on existential philosophy and parenthetically describes his own place within that tradition. The discussion centers about Hirsch's treatment of the thought of Heidegger, a treatment that Tillich holds to be quite unfair. Hirsch condemns Heidegger's work out of hand and, in Tillich's view, he thus fails to show a proper appreciation for Heidegger's valid existential insights. Tillich admits that Heidegger, with his abstract use of concepts, obscures the concrete historical determination of his thought. "But as an existential philosopher he cannot be attacked because of his negativism; for that is an attack upon existential philosophy itself which you formally acknowledge."[31] Tillich elaborates on what he means by this and simultaneously offers a definition of existential philosophy. Existential philosophy, he says, posits existence as a reality lying outside the realm of ideas. There is a dimension of reality that does not yield to logic; it simply is. This aspect of reality cannot be reduced to the content of an idea or a concept. As such it forces man to make decisions; it causes man to struggle; it is the root of uncertainty.[32]

Tillich then cites a number of the leading figures in the existential tradition and specifies points at which each of them discovered "existence." Schelling, for example, recognized the reality of existence in a consideration of the problem of evil. Kierkegaard discovered its presence in the fact of human despair; Marx, in the dehumanizing conditions of the working class. Among contemporary philosophers, Jaspers finds

31. *Ibid.*, 315–16. Cf. *Theology of Culture*, p. 95.
32. Cf. *Theology of Culture*, pp. 87–91.

a peculiar, intractable quality about life in the fact of
mental breakdown. And Heidegger sees a manifesta-
tion of the same thing in man's radical questioning in
face of nothingness. Tillich then adds: "So [too] have
I attempted to develop existential-historical categories
out of an analysis of the threat-character of our
historical existence."[33] All of these men, Tillich argues,
have made a positive contribution to an understanding
of existence, Heidegger included, and the work of
none of them should be blanketed with condemnation.
Hirsch, in his failure to be critical here, shows himself
to be an "enthusiastic idealist," not an "existential
philosopher."[34]

Having outlined in the main sections of the open
letter the matter of Hirsch's dependence upon
Religious-Socialist theory and his use and misuse of the

33. "Die Theologie des Kairos . . . ," 316.
34. Some interpreters of Tillich's thought have suggested
that Heidegger has influenced Tillich in a major way, as, for
example, Bernard Martin, *The Existentialist Theology of
Paul Tillich*, (New York: Bookman Associates, 1963), and
J. Heywood Thomas, *Paul Tillich, An Appraisal*. The present writer is not inclined to deny important influence at
points. This influence appears to have become more extensive
with Tillich's shift away from a primary concern with Religious Socialism and the kairos concept, a shift in emphasis
which can be fixed in the late 1940's. (See below, pp. 95–
100). Tillich's 1944 article, "Existential Philosophy: Its Historical Meaning," included in *Theology of Culture*, seems
to reveal something of a renewed interest in Heidegger's
thought. Martin's judgment that the influence of Heidegger
upon Tillich "has obviously been of a prime order of mag-
nitude" (*op. cit.*, p. 18) lacks the note of moderation that a
study of Tillich's earlier writings demand. To this writer
J. H. Thomas' representation of the influence of Heidegger
upon Tillich is very confused and without value. See Thomas,
pp. 174–175.

kairos concept, Tillich turns a second and concluding section of the letter to consideration of a miscellany of issues posed by Hirsch's book. For example, Tillich is critical of the neglect of a careful sociological analysis of German class structures in Hirsch's appraisal of the political situation. He rejects Hirsch's careless use of the concepts of "folk" and "blood"; he cautions against autocratic and despotic tendencies in Hirsch's theory of the state; and he repudiates the servile role that Hirsch fixes for the Protestant churches within the "totality" of the new German state.

Of all the separate points singled out for special discussion in this second section of the letter, by far the most important theologically and one that again relates directly to the kairos concept is Tillich's analysis of the question of revelation. Tillich accuses Hirsch of setting the events of recent years on the same level as the Biblical documents as a source of revelation. Tillich suggests that it is only because of the Nazi rise to power that Jewish Christians "must" now occupy lesser roles in the German Evangelical Church. And this same fate, Tillich concludes, must inevitably befall all those who do not interpret current political events in the same manner as Hirsch and his German Christian group. The fact that the structure of the church is now redefined on the basis of current political events means, of course, that this group has given these events a new and unusual authority within the church. In the face of this development Tillich asks himself how it is that these ideas are "justified" on the basis of the kairos doctrine. To this self-questioning, Tillich replies by saying: "I do not see how, but I admit that we did not in recent years sufficiently pursue the problems which arise here and that such deviations in interpretation were not clearly excluded."[35] He then says to Hirsch: "In so far as this event [i.e. Hitler's rise to power] and the ramifications of this event in your book force a clarification of these problems, I am, in spite of all [my] criticism, thankful for this."[36] Tillich thereupon offers the following clarification of his views on revelation:

> The concept of revelation has two aspects which must be clearly separated. On the one hand, revelation is reality only as "revelation-correlation." Revelation is not a concept of objectifying thought. Revelation is revelation only when it is realized by some one as such. On the other hand —and this is the second aspect—when revelation is realized correlatively, it is exclusive. There cannot be other revelations beside it. There can only be other situations from which man enters into the revelation-correlation. Every new situation alters the correlation but does not alter the revelation. If I were to express the thing without using the word "revelation" I would speak of "the place" from which our existence receives its unconditional and exclusive, and at the same time, its enduring and determining meaning. Revelation is that to which, as the last criterion of my thinking and acting, I know myself to be unconditionally subjected. The kairos, the historical hour, can therefore never be revelation. It can indicate only the incidence of a new revelation-

35. "Die Theologie des Kairos . . . ," 318.
36. *Ibid.*, 318.

correlation. It designates the moment in which the meaning of revelation for knowing and acting discloses itself anew; it designates the moment in which, for example, the final criterion of truth becomes visible anew over-against a complex of temporal events—the cross of Christ over-against, for example, the demonic character of capitalism or nationalism.[37]

From this elucidation of the relationship of revelation to the kairos concept, Tillich moves on to correct Hirsch's implied definition of revelation as "risk." "Risk," Tillich admits, is involved in the choice of alternatives posed by a new awareness of revelation in a given situation. But revelation is never itself the object of risk. Revelation is the occasion of the assumption of risk in the affirmation of programs and purposes in the political, social, ethical sphere. Risk has its definite place within the kairos situation, but it is not constitutive of the church. No one interpretation of a given historical situation completely exhausts the dimensions of meaning inherent in that situation; therefore, within the church, allowance must always be made for other individuals and groups who appraise the same situation in different ways. Tillich notes that for Hirsch and others of like mind the kairos situation is described as the "German hour," whereas for Tillich and the Religious Socialists it was termed the

37. *Ibid.*, 318. For a later, enlarged statement of this point see Tillich's contribution to the volume entitled *The Kingdom of God and History*, (Chicago: Willett, Clark & Co., 1938), pp. 129–31. The lines of the later "method of correlation" are clearly in evidence here.

"hour of socialism." He further suggests, that for Barth the kairos is interpreted in still another way as "the hour of liberation for the church" in which the centuries-old bourgeois secularization of the church is on the verge of being overthrown. Tillich asserts that all three of these interpretations of the kairos are "risks" that are taken in the present situation but that do not nullify the inclusive fellowship of the church. No one of them is able to concentrate in itself the whole of the great tradition of German theology.

Tillich concludes his discussion of the question of revelation with the observation:

> The decisive thing—and the clear insight into this I owe to opposition to your book—is the fact that revelation and kairos, the pure sense of being grasped and [the reality] of risk, exclusiveness of criterion and relativity of concrete decision—these lie on different levels. Determination by the first makes the theologian a theologian; it provides him with the final criterion. Involvement in the second gives the theologian contemporaneity and historical relevance.[38]

Turning again to Hirsch, Tillich charges: "For the sake of the second [i.e. the kairos] you, in your book have obscured the first [i.e. revelation], and you have done this at a moment when, as a result of the eruption of primitive powers, the Cross as criterion needs

38. *Ibid.*, 319. It is at this point that one can note the clear emergence of the concept of the "theological circle." Cf. *Systematic Theology*, I, pp. 8–11. *Systematic Theology*, II, 14–16.

to be asserted more forcefully than was the case over the past few centuries."[39]

The open letter as a whole is brought to an end with an expression of hope that if the substance of its message could somehow penetrate the consciousness of goodly numbers of Germans the great danger of future disillusionment and suffering would be checked. Tillich suggests to Hirsch, and all others reading the letter, that saving the "fate-afflicted" German people from further suffering would be the greatest service one could perform at this time. Such a service, he asserts, surely supersedes all other philosophical and theological tasks. Then with a concluding formal greeting to Hirsch, the letter is brought to an end.

\* \* \*

The hope with which Tillich concluded his letter was not, of course, realized. Hirsch rejected all remonstrances and persevered in support of the National Socialist cause. He indirectly answered Tillich's "open letter" with a small pamphlet entitled *Christian Freedom and Political Obligation*. Part of the pamphlet was a letter from Hirsch to Dr. Wilhelm Stapel, a leading figure among the German Christians. In the letter to Stapel, Hirsch replied to some of Tillich's criticisms, chiefly to the charge of plagiarism. Tillich, for his part, found significant misunderstanding in Hirsch's interpretation of the original letter, and, in a brief answer in *Theologische Blätter* (May, 1935), he recapitulated the major points. As indicated, however, the original letter and later summary had little or no effect on Hirsch and the German Christians.

39. *Ibid.*, 319.

With regard to the important struggle within the German Evangelical Church during the Nazi years, the German Christian group was never able to establish a position of dominance despite its support by the Nazi Government. The strongest opposition to encroachments upon the freedom and integrity of the Church came from that group within the Church known as the "Confessing Church." Those who comprised this group united behind the "Barmen Declaration" of May 1934, in which statement was made of the essentials of Christian faith over-against Nazi ideology and Nazi interference in church administration. The Confessing Church group, and also the Roman Catholic Church, stood among the few institutions in Nazi Germany that steadfastly opposed the totalitarian pretensions of National Socialism.

It must be said in relation to the German Church struggle that the theology of Paul Tillich did not figure large in the opposition to National Socialism. Much more important in this regard was the point of view of "dialectical theology" represented by Karl Barth. To account for this one must observe that Barth's theology stood much closer to the traditional standards of the church's faith and thus provided a more objective and familiar rallying point than did Tillich's theological-philosophical formulations. Tillich's discovery, in the Hirsch affair, of the need to differentiate more sharply than he had between revelation and the kairos certainly revealed a major flaw in his earlier systematic efforts. Beyond this, however, one must note that the subtleties of Tillich's thought appear to have been too finely drawn to be determinative in the church's fight against National Socialism.

It is ironic that in spite of his own firm stand against Nazism aspects of Tillich's philosophical and theological work lent themselves to the German Christian cause by fixing a source of revelation in general history and therefore in "the natural orders of race, folk, and nation." The Roman Catholic Church, of course, endorsed a "natural revelation," but it is clear that in relation to Nazi Germany its own strong ecclesiastical structure and the loyalty to the institution required of all Catholics provided a base of power and authority capable of effectively withstanding the "enthusiasm of the moment." Tillich, however, in his theoretical labors did not work from such a base. His theological appeal was experienced on a highly intellectual and individualistic level and never reached down into the life of the people at large. This was so in spite of the fact that Tillich and his Religious-Socialist colleagues had sought above all to give expression to the inner longings and aspirations of the laboring man and to formulate the Christian message in the light of his supposed needs.

It was to be expected, in view of all this—the powerful emergence of National Socialism, Tillich's own forced emigration to America, the defection of Hirsch, the collapse of the Religious-Socialist movement—that he himself should give some sort of an appraisal of what had happened. Such an appraisal is to be found in an interesting passage in *The Interpretation of History*, probably written early in 1936. The rather lengthy passage is quoted in full because it represents a difficult grappling on Tillich's part with the meaning of that course of events which seemed to call into question the personal labors of a decade and

91

a half. The passage also represents an alternative interpretation of the collapse of Religious Socialism. In the quotation Tillich gives account of the reasons for his involvement in the German Religious-Socialist movement and the concerns of his post-World War I years down through 1935:

> Not until after the War did the reality and nature of Christian Humanism become totally evident to me. The contact with the Workers Movement, with the so-called de-Christianized masses, revealed clearly to me that here also, within the humanistic form, Christian substance was hidden, even though this Humanism bore the character of a materialistic popular philosophy, long since overcome in art and science. Here Apologetics was even much more difficult, because the religious opposition was made more acute by class opposition. Apologetics, without any regard for this class opposition such as the Church was attempting, was condemned to complete failure from the very beginning. A successful activity on the part of the defenders of Christianity was possible only by their active participation in the class situation, i.e. Apologetics among the proletarian masses was and is possible only to "Religious Socialism." Not Home Missions, but Religious Socialism is the necessary form of Christian activity among proletarian workingmen, and is in particular the necessary form of Christian Apologetics. This apologetic element in Religious Socialism has often been obscured by its political element, so that the Church has never understood

the indirect importance of Religious Socialism for the Church. It was understood much better by the leaders of social democracy, who expressed to me their fear that, as the result of Religious Socialism, the masses might come under the influence of the Church, and thus be alienated from the socialist struggle. A further reason for the repudiation of Religious Socialism by the Church was the fact that Religious Socialism was obliged to discard, or to use only after sufficient preparation, the traditional symbols and concepts of ecclesiastical thought and action. Their use without preparation resulted in an immediate, implicit repudiation on the part of the proletariat. The task was to show that in the peculiar forms of Christian Humanism, as represented by the Workers Movement, the same substance is implied as in the entirely different sacramental forms of the Church. A number of young theologians conceived the situation as I did, and transferred to non-ecclesiastical positions, especially social ones, with the expressed intention of influencing religiously those whom no Church official could reach in any way. Unfortunately, it was not possible to arrange this line of activity in such a way that many might have embraced it. It remained the business of a few. Since, at the same time, the Barthian theology deprived the problem, "Church and Humanistic society," and particularly "Church and Proletariat" of any significance among young theologians, the chasm was never bridged by the Church. The disintegrated humanistic society thus fell victim to a large degree to the new pagan tendencies. The Church was compelled to assemble its defensive resources against these and restrict itself still more anti-humanistically. The proletarian masses sank back again to religious passivity. The intelligentsia now admire the resources which have revealed themselves in the Church contrary to their expectation. They stand aside, however. The gospel for which the Church is fighting does not and cannot touch them. In order to do that the Church would have to proclaim its gospel in a language which could be understood on the soil of the Humanism outside the Church. It would have to give the society, the intelligentsia as well as the masses, the feeling that this gospel is of absolute concern to them. But this feeling cannot be awakened by designedly anti-humanistic paradoxes such as those used in the theology of the Confessional Church.[40]

Such was Tillich's judgment of the situation as he saw it in 1936. And, despite the fact that the years after 1936 did relatively little to reinforce or confirm the theoretical analyses of Religious Socialism, Tillich in principle, though less actively, continued to endorse the Religious Socialist theology of history. After World War II, which confirmed his prediction of tragic disillusionment for the German people, Tillich

40. *Interpretation of History*, pp. 44–46. For a later and somewhat different estimate of these same events see Paul Tillich, "The Present Theological Situation in the Light of the Continental European Development," *Theology Today*, VI, No. 3 (Oct., 1949), 299–310. Cf. also *Systematic Theology*, III, 370–71.

republished in English more of his German writings dealing with the kairos philosophy. These appeared in the collection of essays entitled *The Protestant Era,* published in 1948. In the following year, when asked by the editors of the periodical *The Christian Century* for a statement of how his mind had changed during the decade 1939–49, Tillich reaffirmed his belief in the basic theories of Religious Socialism. He stated then: "I do not doubt that the basic conceptions of religious socialism are valid, that they point to the political and cultural way of life by which alone Europe can be built up."[41]

It is to be noted however that Tillich's statements of 1949 in *The Christian Century* bear a somewhat different quality from the 1936 appraisal of the historical scene. For in 1949, while still affirming "the basic conceptions of religious socialism," he follows that statement with a much less positive observation. He writes: "But I am *not* sure that the adoption of religious-socialist principles is a possibility in any foreseeable future. Instead of a creative *kairos,* I see a vacuum which can be made creative only if it is accepted and endured and, rejecting all kinds of premature solutions, is transformed into a deepening 'sacred void' of waiting."[42] And at another point he confessed that the expectations of a "kairos," a "fulfillment of time," had been "twice shaken, first by the victory of fascism and then by the situation after its military defeat."[43]

41. Tillich, "Beyond Religious Socialism"; *The Christian Century*, LXVI, No. 24 (June 15, 1944), 733.
42. *Ibid.,* p. 733.
43. *Ibid.,* p. 732.

Intimations of a change in emphasis are to be found in these utterances. And Tillich himself gives credence to such a supposition in commenting upon the sub-title of his article: "How My Mind Has Changed in the Last Decade." He asserts in this connection: "It was not a dramatic change in mind that I experienced during the past decade—such a change is hardly to be expected in the sixth decade of one's life—but a slow, often conscious, always effective transformation in various respects."[44] The fact of change is here ac-knowledged, but the nature of the change is not clearly defined. He speaks of the influence of Amer-ica upon his thinking, but refers explicitly only to the discipline of mastering a new language along with the emphasis placed upon social ethics in American theology. As indicated above, he admits to modifica-tions in his social-political expectations. More signifi-cantly he mentions a change in philosophical focus related to the "more recent existential philosophy as developed by Heidegger, Jaspers, and Sartre."[45] And in conjunction with this philosophical note he makes reference to a new and deeper appreciation of the significance of "therapeutic or depth psychology." Of both of these factors, the "more recent existential philosophy" and therapeutic psychology, he writes: "It was partly under this influence that I elaborated my theological system . . . during the past decade."[46]

Here we are brought close to an identification of the one important—though not radical—change in the

44. *Ibid.*
45. *Ibid.*, p. 733.
46. *Ibid.*, p. 733. For another statement of his deepened interest in psychology, see Kegley and Bretall, pp. 18–19.

thought of Tillich over the course of the years after World War I. Father George F. Tavard, an able interpreter of Tillich's thought, has sought to describe the change as a de-emphasis of the kairos concept in favor of the idea of "the New Being in Christ." He describes it as follows:

> Whereas Tillich's pre-war writings highlighted the theme of *kairos*, his writings since then have been focused on the New Being. This is not a contradiction, but a significant evolution. It is as though the kairos which Tillich discerned in the post-World War I period had ended with World War II. . . . His exile in the United States confronted him with a very different social situation. Though still concerned about the *kairos* . . . , he now, and especially in his *Systematic Theology*, laid stress on the trans-historical New Being, *insisting on the ontological more than on the historical dimension of Jesus as the Christ.*[47]

Tavard has obviously made use here of the material Tillich himself supplies in the *Christian Century* article, but he has gone on to add the observation about "kairos" and "New Being" and drawn the parallel with history and ontology. There is, to be sure, a real measure of truth in what Tavard says. In general Tillich's post-World War II writings *do* accent the concept of the New Being and offer fewer attempts to interpret the political-social situation. But the contrast between "kairos" and "New Being" is *not* equivalent to the juxtaposition of an historical and an onto-

47. Tavard, *op. cit.*, p. 112. Italics mine.

logical concern as Tavard suggests. Caution on this point would seem to have been called for by the presence of the concept of "New Being" in some of Tillich's writings of the late 1920's and early 1930's.[48] In fact, as will be shown in the following chapter, ontology underlay Tillich's Religious-Socialist theory from the very start.

As to the matter, however, of the change in Tillich's thought, a most helpful clue is provided by Tillich in his open letter to Hirsch. It will be recalled that in identifying the roots of Hirsch's thought Tillich at one place made a distinction between two types of existentialism: one that derives from the existence of the individual and another that derives from the historical-political situation.[49] He numbered among the individualistic existentialists Kierkegaard, Heidegger, and Jaspers; whereas he listed only Marx—and himself —and Hirsch—as standing for a corporate-historical existentialism (the phrase he used at that time was "existential-historical thought"). One does not want to discount certain polemical features in the open letter to Hirsch, especially Tillich's documentation of Hirsch's indebtedness to Religious Socialism and to Karl Marx. But it is evident that the distinction between an individualistic and a corporate-historical existentialism was at that time a real one. An examination, for example, of the limited use of the phrase "New Being" in *Religious Realization*[50] indicates that the phrase bore at that time important social dimen-

48. See, for example, *Religiöse Verwirklichung*, (Berlin: Furche-Verl., 1930), pp. 29, 41, 59.
49. See above, pp. 75–76.
50. *Religiöse Verwirklichung, op. cit.*

sions and was used in relation to the social-political situation.[51] It should also be noted in this connection that Tillich's dependence upon Heidegger during these earlier years took the form primarily of an adaptation to the realm of corporate existence of Heidegger's individualistic concept of the "threat of nothingness," an adaptation that found expression in Tillich's use of a substitute phrase: the "threat-character" of historical existence (*"Die Bedrohtheit unserer geschichtlichen Existenz"*).[52]

When one recognizes this distinction between an individualistic and a corporate historical existentialism, then Tillich's 1949 discussion of changes in his point of view becomes open to further analysis. When he speaks of his own "religious-socialist attempts" at an existential interpretation of history as "preparing" him for the more recent existential philosophy developed by Heidegger, Jaspers, and Sartre,[53] one is inclined to raise some question with Tillich's use of the word "prepare." It is clear that we have here not simply a transition or an "evolution," as Tavard represents it, but, in the light of Tillich's earlier views, a real change of mind. That it was not in fact a contradiction of his

51. See above, p. 98. n. 48. In passing one might note that a comparison of the corresponding chapters in *Religiöse Verwirklichung* and *The Protestant Era* reveals modifications in other of Tillich's earlier-held views. He omits and modifies in the later work many of his rather doctinaire views on capitalism. He revises passages which may have contributed to Hirsch's National Socialist deviation. And he also moves beyond some of his earlier superficial appraisals of depth psychology.

52. "Die Theologie des Kairos . . . ," 315–316.

53. *The Christian Century*, LXVI, No. 24 (June 15, 1949), 733.

99

kairos philosophy can be explained by the fact that, by means of a distinctive, philosophical definition of man, the definition of man as a microcosm, Tillich was able to shift his emphasis from the macrocosm (in this case the spiritual-historical situation of society at large) to the microcosm (the individual) without essentially revising his basic ontology.[54] But what Tillich did thereby was essentially to abandon his earlier preoccupation with the broad social-political dimensions of history in order to offer a formulation ("New Being") more open to individualistic applications.[55]

This then represents the one notable shift in the thought of Paul Tillich. However the change may be appraised, it is indeed remarkable that over the course of three decades and more, in a world that knew tremendous alteration, one man's thought should show such constancy. Tillich's vision was obviously fixed by something more than the immediacy of events.

54. The idea of man as a microcosm was an early and fundamental tenet of Tillich's thought; it is basic to Tillich's understanding of the relation of the finite to the Infinite, see below p. 109. The fact that Tillich was also early concerned with "justification" and "doubt" (individualistic concerns) indicates that the later shift in emphasis had some precedent.

55. Evidence of deliberation and intent in Tillich's move away from the tenets of Religious Socialism is found in the brief article: "Existentialism and Religious Socialism" in *Christianity and Society*, XV, No 1. (Winter 1949–50), 8–11, esp. 10. As has been suggested, Tillich was far from explicit on the matter of this shift in his thinking: cf. esp. Sydney and Beatrice Rome (eds.), *Philosophical Interrogations* (New York: Holt, Rinehart and Winston, 1964), pp. 404–6. This has required that something more be said.

# IV

## THE ONTOLOGICAL FRAME OF REFERENCE

It has been suggested that the major shift in Tillich's thought is not properly represented as a movement from history to ontology. It is rather to be understood as a shift from an almost exclusive concern with the corporate-historical aspects of human existence to a point of view more inclusive of individualistic dimensions of life. The kairos doctrine is not abandoned; it is definitely retained within the scope of Tillich's system. But in the aftermath of a situation in which the kairos was not properly realized—or in which it was in part erroneously interpreted (a possibility which Tillich foresaw from the start)[1]—there was still something to say to the individual who was seemingly cut adrift in a world without meaning or

1. Tillich, "Kairos," *Die Tat,* XIV (1922), 350. See also *The Protestant Era,* p. 51.

101

direction. This Tillich proceeded to do in the 1950 Terry Lectures at Yale (later published as *The Courage to Be*), in parts of the three volumes of the *Systematic Theology,* and in numerous sermons and articles.

In weighing this change in the course of Tillich's thought a fundamental point to be noted is that it occurred within an ontological frame of reference which had, from first to last, supplied much of the inspiration and determined the character of his thought. Kairos as well as New Being was grounded and rooted in an ontology that was steadfastly maintained throughout Tillich's writings. However much the kairos doctrine may have expressed deep inner emotional drives in Tillich—the revolutionary and romantic motifs—it expressed even more profoundly a body of philosophical ideas essential to his thought as a whole. At the moments of his apparent deepest involvement in the questions of history Tillich was gripped by an even deeper systematic involvement in the questions of ontology. It is therefore not really correct to delineate a historical period in Tillich's thought in contrast to an ontological period (or, for that matter, a philosophical period in contrast to a theological). From the beginning to his death, Tillich was an ontologist of surprisingly uniform persuasion. In order to establish the full nature of this fact and to show its implications for understanding Tillich's systematic endeavors, it is necessary to go back again to the earliest stages of Tillich's thought.

Writing in 1926 at a time when he was apparently

preoccupied with the tenets of Religious Socialism, Tillich observed:

It may be noted that at the present time the metaphysics of being is less highly developed than is the metaphysics of history. The fact is not due to chance. Medieval metaphysics was a metaphysics of being because it arose out of the soil of static, non-historical mysticism. In the Protestant world the dynamic, moving spirit of historical reality has come to prevail in an increasing degree. The meaning of history seems more important to the mind than does the meaning of being.[2]

Significantly, Tillich goes on to remark that: "The metaphysics of history naturally reacts on the metaphysics of being," and he then asserts that the "inner relationship of these two aspects of metaphysical thought" pose a major philosophical problem.[3]

Tillich's own basic metaphysical interest is more clearly shown in a 1924 review of Ernst Troeltsch's important work, *The Historical Standpoint and Its Problems.*[4] In the course of this review Tillich summarily observed that, whereas in Troeltsch's interpretation of history the metaphysical concern was accorded only a secondary place, to Tillich's mind it

2. *The Religious Situation,* (New York: Meridian Books Inc., 1956), p. 81.
3. *Ibid.*
4. Ernest Troeltsch, *Der Historismus und seine Probleme* (Tübingen: Mohr, 1922).

103

should be given primary consideration. As Tillich expressed it:

> But the metaphysical is never an "addition" [to the historical concern]; it is either the foundation or it is nothing. Lacking this, the entire building floats in the air. The word of [strictly] individual creativity can have the effect of destroying creative power if it signifies the demand to compose out of an infinite number of relativities a new relativity—if it does not bear within it a point at which the relative receives its "justification" in the religious sense of the word.[5]

In fact it does not seem too much to say that with Tillich history never was treated simply as history. Tillich was concerned with history, first and foremost, as a vehicle for what he conceived to be its "unconditional" meaning. Ultimately it was *this* that motivated Tillich's long affiliation with Religious Socialism and which lay behind his historical interests to the end.

To see the origin and full dimensions of this metaphysical point of view demands consideration of one of Tillich's earliest works, the 1912 treatise, *Mysticism and Guilt-Consciousness in Schelling's Philosophical Development*. It is this treatise that outlines the ontological boundaries within which Tillich's thought basically moved. It is this work that defines Tillich's philosophical frame of reference. Prepared as a dissertation for the degree of Licentiate of Theology, *Mysticism and Guilt-consiousness* . . . builds upon Tillich's

5. Tillich, "Ernest Troeltsch: Der Historismus und seine Probleme," *Theologische Literaturzeitung*, XLIX, No. 2, (1924), 29.

earlier 1910 study of Schelling's philosophy of religion.[6] The later work however is accorded a fully independent status.[7] Its purpose is to show that the generally accepted assessement of Schelling as a rather impulsive, unstructured, philosophical thinker is quite in error and that there are significant continuities that run throughout the various phases of his thought.[8] Tillich in effect argues that Schelling's philosophical greatness is still fully to be appreciated.

To establish this thesis, Tillich sets about defining the major philosophical problems to which Schelling, along with others of that time, addressed himself. He attempts to show how these problems were previously attacked in the philosophical tradition and how they were finally "solved" by Schelling within what is described as Schelling's "second period," the period of his "positive philosophy." Tillich's analysis falls into three parts: a historical definition of the philosophical problems (which is in part abstracted from Schelling's work as a whole and is a source of confusion and repetition in Tillich's exposition), an analysis of Schelling's early attempts to solve these problems, and finally an account of Schelling's conclusive "solution." A review of these major points, especially the first and the third sets the background of Tillich's own ontology.

\*　　\*　　\*

In the opening paragraph of *Mysticism and Guilt-consciousness* . . . Tillich defines the full import of his

---

6. *Die religionsgeschichtliche Konstruktion in Schellings positiver Philosophie, ihre Voraussetzungen und Prinzipien,* (Breslau: Fleischmann, 1910).
7. *Gesammelte Werke,* I, p. 16.
8. *Ibid.,* pp. 14–15.

study, something not at all apparent from the title of the dissertation:

> Mysticism and guilt-consciousness, feeling of unity with the Absolute and consciousness of opposition to God, the principle of the identity of the absolute and individual spirit and the experience of the contradiction between the holy Lord and the sinful creature: this is an antinomy the solution of which has been earnestly sought by religious thought in the Church down through the centuries—and it must ever again *be* sought. On the one side the will to truth finds satisfaction where the unity of the knower and the object known is attained, where the Absolute is as much the subject of knowledge as the object of knowledge. On the other side, the moral law—where it is grasped in its depth—discloses the God-defying quality of the will, the enmity of the subject towards God.[9]

These two conflicting aspects of human experience are reflected, Tillich suggests, in the Greek philosophical vision of eternal, self-contained truth, and in the picture of the holy and exalted God of Israel, whose countenance is a consuming fire. These symbols represent in broad feature a long-standing tension between truth and morality in Western thought. The tension is such that where one element is stressed the other is in constant danger of dissolution. Thus, during the nineteenth century, for example, Hegel laid such emphasis upon the idea of truth that the ethical cate-

9. *Ibid.,* p. 17.

gories were ignored and Christianity as a religion was all but severed from its common moral ties with Judaism. At the same time, however, there were others (Harnack, Herrmann, Kaftan) who accented the moral categories and deprecated the influence of Greek thought and Greek mysticism upon the history of the Church. In the light of this oscillating pattern, Tillich asks whether Schelling may perhaps have achieved a meaningful synthesis of mysticism and guilt, truth and morality.

What Tillich initiates is in effect an introduction to the tradition of ontology. Since "being" (Greek: *on*, *ontos*) is the term that embraces all reality, the science or "logos" of being, ontology, is the attempt to establish the unity and coherence of reality in the face of disruptive cleavages in man's experience of reality. As a first step in defining such a science of being there is the necessity of identifying a specific pattern of contradiction or incongruity as a prelude to the formulation of a "principle of identity" by which the contradiction is overcome. In the case of Schelling—and Tillich—interest is initially focused on two forms of the principle of identity which arose in answer to separate patterns of disparity. The first and older principle of identity is described as the Socratic principle; the second, as the Augustinian.

In the case of the Socratic principle, address was made to the problem of "the one and the many," and a "solution" to the problem was found by presupposing the reality of the idea or concept. Ideas were accorded degrees of reality proportionate to their capacity to embrace multiplicity; thus the more comprehensive an idea was thought to be, the more real it was also believed to be since it was able to encompass a larger measure of particular existence. Truth, in relation to this form of the principle of identity, was equated with the process of generalization, the movement from the particular to the general, reaching a culmination in the idea of "the Good" (Plato) or "the One" (Plotinus). At the final stage of "the Good" or "the One" the individual who sought a vision of pure and perfect truth was called upon to turn away from every form of particular, conditioned existence, even the individual's own existence, to experience, through "ecstasy," union with the final reality.[10]

It is to be noted that there is in this early "Socratic" formula no sense of conflict between a subjective and an objective world. Ideas were simply assumed to possess objective reality. This is not the case however with the Augustinian principle of identity, which regarded the cleavage between subject and object as the fundamental split in reality. In this instance the subject, doubting all objects and the external world in general, sought certainty on the basis of his own subjective mental processes.[11] The result was that truth in the Augustinian tradition was conceived to be inseparable from the self-certainty of the subject. Such, for example, is the import of Descartes' assertion: " I think, therefore I am." And the same motif is found in Malebranche's severance of the external world from subjective consciousness, his lack of concern with the

10. *Ibid.*, pp. 18-19.
11. That there may also be certain Socratic motifs in this form of the principle of identity is not discussed by Tillich. Socrates did, after all, espouse a pattern of questioning and systematic doubt in quest of inner certainty.

external world as such, and the assertion of unbroken continuity between the individual spirit and universal "Spiritual Substance."[12]

Tillich notes that it is this second form of the ontological problem, the dichotomy of subject and object, that has generally most concerned modern Western philosophy. He observes however that there were, during the late Middle Ages and on into the eighteenth century, some influential and fruitful syntheses of the two forms of identity. The enunciation, during the Middle Ages, of the principle of the "coincidence of opposites"—the idea that every contrast presupposes an underlying unity on the basis of which the contrast is drawn—worked towards a synthesis of the "One" of Plotinus and the Augustinian emphasis upon individual, subjective self-awareness. The "One" was taken up into the concept of "the Infinite," which in turn was interpreted as a qualitative, subjective concept. Every finite thing, by virtue of its subjectivity, was interpreted as participating in the Infinite, and the Infinite was regarded as implicit in everything finite. Thus with Nicholas Cusanus and Giordano Bruno everything became in some degree a mirror of the Universal, a microcosm, with man as its most complete expression. It was Leibniz who brought this line of thinking to its final development in the concept of the monad. "The monad is identity of subject and object, of oneness and multiplicity, of the Infinite and the finite."[13] In Leibniz, Tillich observes: "The act of per-

12. *Ibid.*, p. 18. Tillich suggests, incidentally, that the Judeo-Christian sense of guilt gave special potency to the subject-object dichotomy.
13. *Ibid.*, p. 19.

ception is a purely subjective event, a coming to consciousness of the monad without external influence."[14] It is clear that in this pattern of thought the classical Greek concern is manifested in the tendency to conceive truth in the context of the "One" and the Augustinian motif is to be discerned in the effort to overcome doubt by turning away from the external world to subjective assurance.

If this particular Leibnizian synthesis of the two forms of the principle of identity found expression in an accent upon the individual, upon man as a microcosm, there was a second, equally significant synthesis, which underlined the universal, macrocosmic point of view. Leibniz's synthesis reflected an Augustinian bias; Spinoza's revealed the influence of Greek universalism. In Spinoza's concept of "Absolute Substance" the individual as such disappears. "Substance" is interpreted as embracing the attributes of thought and extension, ideality and reality, subjectivity and objectivity. Thus the dichotomy of subject and object, along with that of the one and the many, is taken up into and resolved within an all inclusive Absolute.

The fact, however, that two differing patterns of ontological thought persisted into the eighteenth century suggested the need of further development. This was also called for by an increasing philosophical concern with the question of morality, a matter not adequately represented by the dichotomies of the one and the many, subject and object. Tillich points out that when the relationship to God is viewed primarily in terms of the question of truth inevitably some pattern

14. *Ibid.*

110

of identity is assumed, some affinity between the divine and the human spirit. This constitutes the root of the mystical religious tradition. When, however, a relationship to God is viewed principally in moral terms then it is possible to assert, as Kierkegaard did, that "the normal behaviour of men towards God is repentance."[15] The idea of repentance here bears important ontological implications. It means that sin cannot be interpreted simply as a deficiency in man, something that can be overcome in process. Sin is strictly an "ought-not-to-be" that should not be given a necessary function within the scheme of thesis-antithesis-synthesis. To do so is to grant sin a measure of positive value, even if only as an obstacle to be overcome in the movement towards a higher synthesis. Evaluations of this sort finally rule out the concept—and reality—of guilt and repentance. They finally speak for the union of the unholy will with the Holy God and annul the distinction between good and evil. Tillich concludes, with Schelling, that he who knows God as "holy" experiences the separation between God and man as "divine wrath and human guilt." In this situation the consciousness of guilt frequently becomes "the religious expression for the absolute antithesis between God and man."[16]

Stepping back, as it were, to assess this picture of ontological conflict, Tillich observes that the two traditions of mysticism and guilt appear to be in absolute contradiction. He suggests however that a careful examination of both standpoints reveals antinomies within each which rule out such absolute opposition.

15. *Ibid.*, pp. 20–21.
16. *Ibid.*, pp. 21–22.

First, in the matter of truth, although affirming that identity rightly underlies the idea of truth, Tillich suggests that it is wrong to assume that truth and reality are identical. Reality is actually a more comprehensive term than truth and this fact, he argues, is amply attested by the tradition itself. Citing some of the classic figures in the tradition, Tillich observes that all of them took note of a "something" that is not assimilated by reason. Plato and Aristotle, for example, both asserted that matter was never completely overcome in union with the idea. Plotinus insisted on the necessity of a "leap," a movement beyond reason, in man's final ascent to the "One." Nicholas Cusanus declared that the equation of the Infinite and the finite could never be fully achieved and that allowance had to be made for a "learned ignorance."[17] Similarly, Leibniz spoke of "the muddled concept" and the "necessity of deficiency." Thus, in surveying the over-all course of the tradition of "truth mysticism," Tillich asserts that the "entire standpoint falls into a split between a true godly reality and an untrue god-forsaken reality. Identity with God and godlessness alternate: the unity of the religious life is threatened."[18]

But if the mystical tradition is burdened with a noticeable antinomy, so also is that of morality and guilt-consciousness. Here Tillich, abstracting from the work of Schelling, makes use of the principle of the coincidence of opposites and argues that no matter how great the opposition between God and man is conceived to be, the relationship between them is never wholly destroyed. "Opposition can only be as-

17. Cf. *S.T.* I, pp. 81–82.
18. *Gesammelte Werke*, I, p. 22.

serted so long as both parties are forced to be 'at one and the same place'. . . . What has absolutely no mutuality, no moment of identity, cannot stand in contradiction."[19] Indeed, Tillich concludes, "Logically considered the greatest antithesis is possible only where the greatest identity is present. . . ."[20] Against Kierkegaard he therefore asserts: "So then, there is also, in the long run, no piety whose normal behavior is repentance."[21]

Following this introductory analysis of the problems of ontology, Tillich proceeds to analyze the ontological contributions of Immanuel Kant, for it is Kant who provides the immediate background for Schelling's work. Kant, it will be recalled, was "roused from his philosophical slumbers" by the work of David Hume. As Locke had undertaken to criticize the philosophical concept of substance, so Hume challenged the assumption that the idea of causality was derived from the observation of objective phenomena. The idea of causality, Hume suggested, could well be simply a habit of mind, quite independent of events "out there." Tillich observes that this course of thought seriously threatened the idea of truth by drawing a line between the functions of consciousness and real events. He remarks:

> It was at this point that Kant stepped in: his "Critique of Pure Reason" is a struggle for identity and truth against positivism and scepticism. He allowed Hume his presupposition, but denied

19. *Ibid.*
20. *Ibid.*
21. *Ibid.*, p. 23.

him the right to distinguish from the perceptible
world, formed through the functions of consciousness, an objective concept of things. He ad-
mitted that identity is never to be proved if at
the outset the subject and object are torn apart,
but he denied the right of this separation. In the
functions of reason and the space/time categories reason is a thing unto itself; but, as such, it
is at the same time bound up with things, for
things are found nowhere else but in the world
of appearance formed by the functions of consciousness.[22]

Tillich asserts that here "the last dogma which Hume
had allowed to stand and on the basis of which he had
grounded his positivism, the dogma of a cleavage between subject and object, is removed; and the idea of
truth is more firmly established than before."[23] Here
both the Socratic form of the principle of indentity
and the Augustinian principle are given expression in
the concept of synthesis, for, according to Kant,
"consciousness is nothing other than an act of the synthesis of multiplicity, and all modes of the understanding are forms of comprehending multiplicity in the
unity of consciousness. Truth is the identity of the
multiplicity of the object in the unity of the subject."[24]

But Kant, like those before him, did not reduce his
understanding of reality to the principle of identity.
He included within his purview the concept of the
*Ding an sich*, the "thing-in-itself." This Tillich inter-

22. *Ibid.*, p. 24.
23. *Ibid.*
24. *Ibid.*, p. 25.

prets as a "boundary concept," a limit set to the identity of subject and object, of unity and multiplicity. As a "boundary concept" the "thing-in-itself" does not hold out the possibility of a more adequate objective idea of things. It simply marks a limit. In short, Kant denied with this concept the possibility of an absolute, completed synthesis. He affirmed only individual acts of the synthesizing consciousness. "Truth inheres in the act of synthesis; but this is precisely its relativity, for if it were perfect, it would not be in need of actuality."[25] Kant offered no answer to those who ask, how is it possible that reason has this limitation?—what is the relation of the "thing-in-itself" to the world of appearance? Tillich suggests that one has at this point an important source of irrationality in the development of idealism.

Kant's broad philosophical perspective was of course not limited to the question of truth, or the *Critique of Pure Reason*. Sensitive to the growing concern with morality, Kant gave attention to this subject in his *Critique of Practical Reason*. The discussion here centered chiefly around two concepts: autonomy and freedom. The former concept, autonomy, embodies still another form of the principle of identity and is given application in Kant's representation of the moral law. Following a lead of Spinoza, Kant defined autonomy as freedom from external constraint. Freedom from external constraint, however, does not mean arbitrariness. "Autonomy" bears the literal meaning of a "law of self." The moral law, Kant argued, represents the true nature of the human self and as such is not to be conceived as an alien de-

25. *Ibid.*

mand, a form of external constraint. To act in conformity with the moral law is in fact to fulfill the law of the self and realize humanity. What seemingly comes from outside as the sense of "ought" is actually only the call to be oneself.

This definition of the moral law did not, of course, explain the fact of evil. Why is it that man fails so often to fulfill the law of self? In answer to this question, Kant in another work, *Religion within the Limits of Reason Alone*, suggested that man has the capacity also to decide against himself, to contradict himself. Besides autonomy, which Tillich refers to as "material freedom," man is possessed of "formal freedom," the possibility of self-contradiction.[26] In possession of "formal freedom" man is able to violate his own nature and do evil. And it is at this point that Kant introduced his doctrine of "radical evil." "Radical evil" is the propensity of man to decide against reason, against the moral law, a decision resulting in a disruption of the proper relation of reason to nature. Nature usurps reason's role and man becomes subject to his passions. So widespread was this phenomenon that Kant came to regard "radical evil" as a condition of all men, an all-pervasive "transcendental decision" against reason. With this latter step, Tillich points out, Kant in effect undermined his previously defined pattern of identity (autonomy): if radical evil is accorded a dominant role in empirical man—in place of autonomy and the moral law—it becomes impossible to see how a relationship of harmony with the moral law can be reestablished. In a situation of "radical evil" one cannot regard a man as morally good in

26. *Ibid.*, p. 29.

116

some actions, while at the same time being evil in others.[27] Such unresolved tension in Kant's moral philosophy pointed inevitably to the need of a more adequate representation of man's moral situation—a task which Schelling eventually assumed.

It was, in fact, in a third phase of Kant's thought, the *Critique of Judgment,* that Schelling found the beginnings of a "solution" to a wide range of ontological questionings, among them the moral question. The material for this solution lay hidden, Tillich says, under an overlay of "schematic" and "hypothetical" formulations, but in the *Critique of Judgment* the principle of identity scored, in Tillich's words, a "surprising triumph." Here also the "intuitive understanding" came into its own.

All judgment, Tillich points out, expresses the classical Greek idea of identity, the subsumption of the particular under the general. However in the sphere of "aesthetic judgment," there is also significant expression of a balance between two other factors, necessity and freedom. The argument runs as follows. The recognition of beauty is the intuitive perception of a harmony between certain general rules of beauty, rooted in a supra-individualistic "general consciousness," and a particular sensible object. Though the judgment that a thing is beautiful is not demonstrable or provable, it can nevertheless be shared by other persons because it is grounded in an a priori function of the human spirit. Discussion of the aesthetic judgment however is not limited simply to a *recognition* of a correspondence and harmony that exists already at hand. It involves also the production of a harmony

27. *Ibid.,* p. 30.

that did not previously exist. In art there is an actualization of beauty, a realization of the general in the particular through the agency of man's freedom. (This is true also of purposeful activity in other areas of life.) Thus on the one hand aesthetic judgment expresses recognition of a beauty that already exists in an object on the basis of necessity; and, on the other hand, in art, it leads to the realization of beauty on the basis of freedom. Kant was therefore able to assert that the artistic genius accomplishes on the basis of freedom what nature produces on the basis of necessity.[28]

The description of this parallelism between necessity and freedom, between human passivity and human activity vis-à-vis the world, is clearly for both Schelling and Tillich one of Kant's most germinal ideas. The dichotomy is eventually transposed by Schelling into a lower and higher order of existence in connection with the definition of a dynamic ontology. But before attaining this "second" or "positive" stage of his thought, Schelling spent many years and devoted numerous writings to an exploration of particular forms of identity in the areas of the will, nature, art, and the "intellectual intuition." Tillich, in point of fact, sets apart the whole of the second section of *Mysticism and Guilt-Consciousness* . . . to an exposition of this phase of Schelling's work, a study that reveals interesting points of contact with some of Tillich's later formulations. A recapitulation, however, of this particular portion of Tillich's discussion is not essential to the presentation of a broad picture of Til-

28. *Ibid.*, p. 33.

118

lich's ontological frame of reference and therefore can be passed over. It is to the third and final section of *Mysticism and Guilt-Consciousness* . . . , the presentation of Schelling's "positive philosophy," that we therefore turn.

\* \* \*

Schelling's early attempts to define "closed," all-encompassing systems of identity in the areas of will, nature, art, and intellectual intuition continually encountered unresolved tensions that drove him on successively to new formulations. In each of the aforementioned spheres some sort of final dilemma wrote an end to his attempt to establish a completed synthesis. The impossibility of eliminating the irrational in life, dissatisfaction with the formula of "autonomy" as a definition of human freedom, and a growing, deep-rooted unease in the face of superficial, bourgeois morality: these matters eventually led Schelling to a reappraisal of the idea of God.

In moving towards this reappraisal Schelling repudiated the Kantian and post-Kantian attempts to establish the idea of God on the basis of man's moral sense. He condemned the wide company of "Malvolios" who "suppose that because they are virtuous there should no longer be any beauty, any excellence of 'Nature' "[29] and declared it a "horror to want to deduce God from morality, to make the human deed primary and God secondary. Basically it is a denial of the grace of God."[30] God, Schelling finally asserted, is the all-embracing reality; God himself is the final synthesis, the One who contains within Himself

29. *Ibid.*, p. 48.
30. *Ibid.*

119

both reason and the irrational, essence and existence. As Tillich describes Schelling's thought at this point:

> The more essence, the greater the contradiction, the higher the synthesis; in the absolute Synthesis essence eternally asserts itself against absolute contradiction, freedom against necessity, the rational against the irrational, light against darkness: but this synthesis is God.[31]

In Schelling's positive philosophy God is "not only an eternal being, but an eternal becoming."[32] God is a coming-to-consciousness whose beginning lies in the moment when "He separates himself from himself, sets himself against himself, . . . not in order to remain with this opposition but in order to lead darkness into light. . . ."[33] God transcends the cleavage of subject and object. He subordinates the sphere of objectivity, causality, and necessity to his own purpose of "leading darkness into light." Thus the basically static ontology of truth mysticism gives way to a dynamic ontology. Tillich concludes:

> Only he who clings to the abstract concept of the *ens realissimum* . . . can overlook this opposition of the rational and the irrational in God, can forget that without opposition there is no life, that every thing, in order to manifest itself, needs something that is, in the strict sense, not itself.[34]

31. *Ibid.*, p. 79.
32. *Ibid.*, p. 80.
33. *Ibid.*
34. *Ibid.*

In whatever way one appraises this formula—and one must say that it bears a certain "intuitive" quality—one must note that in Schelling's "positive philosophy" stress falls upon awareness of a living God. By following the canons of reason, the necessities of logic, one can, Schelling agreed, arrive at the idea of the Absolute, but reason, he insisted, cannot establish the reality of the "living God." To want to do this through reason is in fact to want to reduce freedom to necessity, a course to be rejected. He declared rather that God, who bears within himself all contradiction, is essentially will and act. God spontaneously and creatively pursues His purposes, and man must follow God in His acts if he would know Him.

Such ideas were bound to raise the charge of humanizing the Absolute, but Schelling stood his ground:

> Against the attempt to counter him with the reproach of unfounded anthropomorphism Schelling stressed and justified the irrational character of the way from the Absolute to God, "If He [the Absolute] is now human, who will take exception to that?" It is not permissible to ascribe something to God *a priori*. The task of theology is only to follow His course. "He is what He wills to be. Therefore I must first seek to discern His will, not however to restrain Him beforehand from being what He wills to be." Overagainst the irrational one must [simply] observe and experience. Existence can be proved in no other way than through itself.[35]

35. *Ibid.*, p. 86. Although there is seemingly offered here the possibility of introducing a "heteronomous" revelation and an authoritative Scripture, it is clear that Schelling and

Thus impelled, Schelling moved on in his analysis from the realm of reason to that of history. Since God is also an unfolding of personality in act and deed, it is necessary to look to history for expression of other features of God's being and person. And Schelling believed that this was especially manifested in the Christian revelation. In the Cross he felt he discerned the reality of both God's wrath and grace. To explain his meaning Schelling entered into a treatment of the complex question of sin.

In connection with this difficult and crucial phase of Schelling's thought, it is essential to understand that he did not identify sin with the basic "contradiction" that exists within God. Sin, Schelling insisted, is not equivalent to that "negative principle" which is fundamental to the assertion of a dynamic, living process. For Schelling to have made such an identification would, of course, have provided sin once more with a *necessary* place within the scheme of things, thus destroying the sense of guilt that Schelling tried to preserve against a variegated contemporary pattern of moralism and popular belief in progress. At most, the principle of contradiction within God affords a ground for human sin; it is not itself sin. Particularity, individual existence, is an expression of God's "separation of himself from himself," a necessity of existence. But individuality is also eternally assimilated again into the universal will and purpose of God. Each and every individual ought properly to realize reunion with the

Tillich do not follow this course. In ascribing will to God what is important for both Schelling and Tillich is the idea of a continuing and active synthesizing function for God in the process of history.

Absolute. In the divine there is a movement toward differentiation, but also a movement of return and reunion.[36] This process is fundamental. Sin, however, enters as a disruption of this process. Man, the epitome of the created order, possessed of will and freedom, goes beyond the simple and positive affirmation of individuality and makes himself "the center of his world" (as Tillich later expressed it). Man can oppose a return to his ultimate Ground and thereby deny his finitude. As Tillich summarizes Schelling: "Sin is the attempt of the individual to set himself against the process of the re-absorption (*Wiederaufhebung*) of all individuals into the unity of the Absolute Synthesis. . . . Sin is selfhood which wants to elevate itself as selfhood."[37] This is, according to Schelling, "not lack of Spirit, but perversion of Spirit."[38] It is a free act on the part of man; and this, then, becomes the source of the sense of guilt, the occasion for repentance. In repentance man properly reaffirms his indestructible bond with Eternal Being—a bond known not only through the logic of the "coincidence of opposites,"[39] but also manifest in God's act in Christ.

According to Schelling, evil is inextricably bound up with good. It preys upon good and has no full-standing reality of its own. "For evil, when it is entirely separated from good, no longer exists . . . as evil. It can only operate through (violated) good. . . . The end of revelation is therefore the casting out of evil

36. Cf. *Ibid.*, pp. 61, 98.
37. *Ibid.*, p. 89.
38. *Ibid.*, p. 90.
39. *Ibid.*, p. 93. See above, p. 27 n. 23.

from good, the declaration of evil as total unreality."[40] This God Himself accomplishes. Tillich again quotes Schelling:

> As selfhood [emersed] in evil makes the light, or the word, its own and thus appears as a higher ground of darkness, so must the word spoken in opposition to the evil in the world accept humanity, or selfhood, and itself become personal. . . . Only the personal can sanctify the personal and God must become man, in order that man comes again to God. . . .[41]

Schelling averred that communion with God is possible only if God himself becomes individual personality. The irrational in all of its immediacy, the individuality of human personality, becomes the occasion of "the eternal personalization of the Absolute." The end and purpose of the incarnation of God is not to justify selfhood in its perverted form but to judge the same through the Cross. At the Cross the one will which was justified in a claim of absoluteness offered itself up in sacrifice. "The truly Infinite comes into the finite, not in order to deify the finite, but in order for God to sacrifice this in his own person and thereby make reconciliation."[42] Every pretension of man is thereby ruled out, while human life is affirmed in its goodness. The Cross of Christ is thus seen also as the grace of God: the affirmation of the finite self within

40. *Ibid.*, p. 95.
41. *Ibid.*, p. 96.
42. *Ibid.*, p. 97.

the compass of God's infinite presence and on-going purpose.

Following exposition of the meaning of the "Son," Schelling brought his "positive philosophy" to a close with a very important and illuminating description of the Spirit's role in the movement of history. "Spirit," Schelling suggested, is God's on-going struggle against perverted selfhood; it is a movement beyond repentance (recognition of the "ought-not-to-be") to an affirmation and realization of the "ought-to-be." With every phase of the historical process new values, new "ideas," new "syntheses" emerge; and all men are called to share in their realization. Necessarily one synthesis will displace another in the course of time. The Spirit is dynamic; it cannot be contained within a single synthesis. Thus, room must always be made for a new idea, a new ordering and containment of multiplicity. Within each and every such synthesis there is the presence, but not the fullness, of the Absolute.[43] True religion, Schelling held, was nothing other than the Spirit manifesting itself dynamically through human consciousness and achievement.

\* \* \*

Thus did Schelling, in Tillich's view, break through the confines of statically conceived systems of identity and set forth a new, dynamic ontology in which freedom, irrationality, and guilt are given their due. A quest for identity that had begun with man's attempts to *define* truth is brought to an end with a call to man to *do* the truth. Contemplation and quietism are replaced by a sense of individual participation in the

43. *Ibid.*, pp. 99–100.

divine process of history. Through the acceptance of finitude and creative endeavor man's true being is realized, reconciliation with God achieved.

That Tillich came to speak of kairos was not alone the outgrowth of a shattering world war; it arose also —one can say: "in the first instance"—out of commitment to the questions and answers of ontology defined by his early study of Schelling.

# V

## EXPOSITION OF THE *Systematic Theology*

In a number of works composed after World War I, Tillich showed his involvement with the onto-logical problems and some of the solutions to those problems which his earlier study of Schelling had provided. In the 1922 lecture "Overcoming the Concept of Religion in the Philosophy of Religion", Tillich argued for the necessity of transcending the objectifying, cultic tendencies of religion through awareness of the "unconditional Ground" of all culture. In *The System of the Sciences.* . . . (1923) he sought to order hierarchically the various types and methods of knowledge according to the measure of detachment governing the relation between the subject and the object of knowledge. And in the essay, "Kairos und Logos" (1926) he attempted to reconcile the static qualities of truth with the dynamic movement of history. As previously stated, these systematic

127

ontological interests were not something "along side of," or "in addition to," Tillich's Religious Socialism. They represented an essential ground of Religious Socialism, and they stand witness to the fact that World War I actually seemed to reinforce and deepen important patterns of thought expressed earlier.

It would be quite possible to elaborate in detail the lines of ontological continuity between the early 1912 study of Schelling and Tillich's post-World War I writings. As valuable as this endeavor might prove to be at some points, an ultimately more useful enterprise—and one more basic to a definition of Tillich's enduring intellectual concerns—is a description of how the ontological formulae of *Mysticism and Guilt-consciousness* . . . find expression in and help illumine Tillich's definitive work, the three volume *Systematic Theology* (1951–1963). To proceed along these latter lines is actually to set forth most sharply the import of what Tillich wrote in 1949: "Above all I have come to realize that a few great and lasting things are decisive for the human mind, and that to cling to them is more important than to look for dramatic changes."[1]

*     *     *

In the *Systematic Theology*, as in *Mysticism and Guilt-consciousness* . . . , one is inescapably confronted with Tillich's ontological concern for divisions, splits, apparent contradictions in man's experience of reality. The list of these divisions and dichotomies is extended and broadened in his later work, but the basic character of those identified in

1. "Beyond Religious Socialism," *The Christian Century*, (1949), LXVI, 733.

*Mysticism and Guilt-consciousness* . . . is everywhere apparent. The subject-object dichotomy is carried over, but it is also given further expression in such polar pairings as "self-world" and "dynamics-form." The cleavage between the one and the many is represented in terms of the polarity of "participation" (the principle of unity) and "individuation" (an expression of manifoldness). "Freedom and destiny" takes up the earlier contrasts of freedom and necessity and freedom and fate.

Not only are all the earlier divisions and cleavages present in the *Systematic Theology*, as a matter of course the basic ontological purpose of reconciling the cleavages, eliminating the conflicts, ordering the unordered, remains the same. In terms of the earlier study this is the quest for "principles of identity" to bridge the cleavages and unite disparate elements. Such is clearly *a* major, if not *the* major, purpose and goal of the *Systematic Theology*—depending upon how one also weighs the closely related and long-standing apologetic concern which Tillich sets forth in the Introduction to the *Systematic Theology*.[2]

Methodologically there are in the *Systematic Theology* two important "solutions" to the problem of ontological conflict, solutions that are first suggested in *Mysticism and Guilt-consciousness* . . . and variously applied in the later work. The first of these methodological principles is that of hierarchical ordering, the definition of lower and higher levels of being that rule out essential conflict between factors of different "levels." Hierarchical ordering follows the

2. *Systematic Theology*, I, pp. 3–8.

lines of the early Socratic principle of identity in union with the later tradition of Cusanus, Bruno, and Leibniz.[3] In the first volume of the *Systematic Theology*, Tillich refers to this approach as "gradualistic metaphysics." He describes it in the following terms:

> Ever since Plato wrote his *Symposium* and Aristotle his *Metaphysics* this type of thinking has influenced the Western world in many ways. The absolute is the highest in a scale of relative degrees of being (Plotinus, Dionysius, the Scholastics). The nearer a thing or a sphere of reality is to the absolute, the more being is embodied in it. God is the highest being . . . Leibniz's monadology is an outstanding example of hierarchical thinking in modern philosophy. The degree of conscious perception determines the ontological status of a monad, from the lowest form of being to God as the central monad. The romantic philosophy of nature applies the hierarchical principle to the different levels of the natural and the spiritual world. It is a triumph of hierarchical thinking that evolutionary philosophers since Hegel's time have employed the formerly static degrees of being as standards of progress in their schemes of dynamic development.[4]

3. See above, pp. 109–110. It should be pointed out that this "solution" finds extensive expression in Schelling's "Nature Mysticism" (cf. *Gesammelte Werke*, I, pp. 42–7), in which the traditional philosophical juxtaposition of "Nature" and "Spirit," "body," and "mind," is eliminated.
4. *Systematic Theology*, I, p. 233.

Tillich's own use of this hierarchical principle, especially in its dynamic form, is apparent at various points in the *Systematic Theology*. Its most obvious application is found in the description of the relationship of human life to other realms of being, both inorganic and organic. In offering justification of the designation of higher and lower "dimensions" of life, Tillich states that the criteria for such gradation are:

> . . . the definiteness of the center, on the one hand, and the amount of content on the other. . . . They decide the establishment of the animal dimension above the dimension of the vegetative. They decide that the dimension of inner awareness surpasses the biological and is surpassed by the dimension of the spirit. They decide that man is the highest being because his center is all-embracing. In contrast to all other beings, man does not have only environment; he has world, the structured unity of all possible content. This and its implications make him the highest being.[5]

The "ontological" motivation of such an hierarchical scheme, the exclusion of conflict, is strikingly stated in the course of Tillich's rather forced criticism of the use of the term "level" in traditional philosophical thought. To Tillich "level" suggests the idea of isolation and a lack of participation of one level of being in another. As he says, "There is no organic movement from one to the other; the higher is not implicit in the lower and the lower is not implicit in

5. *Systematic Theology*, III, p. 36.

the higher."[6] Therefore, as a substitute for the word "level" Tillich proposes use of the term "dimension":

> The metaphor "dimension" is also taken from the spatial sphere, but it describes the difference of the realms of being in such a way *that there cannot be mutual interference;* depth does not interfere with breadth, since all dimensions meet in the same point. They cross without disturbing each other; *there is no conflict between dimensions.* Therefore the replacement of the metaphor "level" by the metaphor "dimension" represents an encounter with reality in which *the unity of life is seen above its conflicts.* These conflicts are not denied, but they are not derived from the hierarchy of levels; they are consequences of the ambiguity of all life processes and are therefore conquerable without the destruction of one level by another. They do not refute the doctrine of the multidimensional unity of life.[7]

Quite apart from the question of the merit of Tillich's argument about "levels" and "dimensions," it is evident that Tillich himself does *not* reject the principle of hierarchical ordering as such. Rather, he is very much at pains to preserve the principle, with the proviso that room be made for the implicit participation of each level of being in every other level of being. Hierarchical ordering is a chief means by which Tillich maintains the coherence and unity of being

6. *Ibid.,* p. 13.
7. *Ibid.,* p. 15. Italics mine.

against the threat of any form of metaphysical dualism.[8]

There is, however, a second method or principle nascent in the early study of Schelling that Tillich also uses to eliminate ontological conflict. This second ontological formula can be described as the principle of polarization. As an adaptation of the all-important doctrine of the coincidence of opposites, it represents a much more difficult principle to delimit and interpret than the previously described hierarchical principle. This arises from the fact that polarization is used by Tillich in subtly different ways, with varying ontological implications. Frequently it takes on some of the coloration of hierarchical ordering, but in the main polarization implies a balance between two separate but related elements. In expanding, for example, upon the complementary idea of "correlation," Tillich speaks of "a unity of the dependence and independence of two factors."[9] And at another point, he describes a polarity as a relationship in which "Each pole is meaningful only in so far as it refers by implication to the opposite pole."[10] Application of this

8. For other expressions of the hierarchical principle, see *Systematic Theology*, I, 62–3, 170–71, 175–76, 180; *Systematic Theology*, II, 42–3, 120–21; *Systematic Theology*, III, 17, 53–4, 84, 376–77.

9. *Systematic Theology*, II, 13.

10. *Systematic Theology*, I, 165. The idea of polarity, growing out of the coincidence of opposites, certainly underlies at points Tillich's use of the term "dialectics"; see *Systematic Theology*, II, 90. In this reference, however, as elsewhere, there is expression also of the Hegelian dialectic, the movement from thesis to its negation and on to a new thesis (or synthesis); cf. *Systematic Theology*, I, 234–35, *Systematic*

133

principle is especially apparent in Tillich's pairing of the fundamental ontological elements—individuation and participation, dynamics and form, freedom and destiny. In each instance Tillich is able to nullify an absolute contradiction or antithesis between the polar elements by arguing that neither element is what it is apart from its polar opposite. In point of fact, not only is the antithesis nullified, attention is directed to a unifying ground which underlies each and all polarities. In this latter feature approach is made to Schelling's declaration that God must be viewed as a "synthesis" rather than a "thesis." Tillich gives expression to this view when he writes: "The polar character of the ontological elements is rooted in the divine life, every ontological element includes its polar element completely, without tension and without threat of dissolution, for God is being-itself."[11]

The complications surrounding Tillich's use of the principle of polarization are illustrated by what Tillich goes on to say immediately following the preceding description of polar balance within being-itself:

---

*Theology*, III, 329. But the coincidence of opposites and Hegel's dialectic are not identical. Unfortunately Tillich does not deal with this matter.

11. *Systematic Theology*, I, 243. Tillich's statement about the role of polarity in Schelling's thought is not, to the mind of this interpreter, wholly conclusive: cf. Sydney and Beatrice Rome, *op. cit.*, pp. 358–59. Tillich has undoubtedly developed the concept of polarity to a degree not found in Schelling, but it must also be said that Schelling's idea of God as "synthesis" points in this direction. Certainly polarization is an outgrowth of the "coincidence of opposites," a principle with which Schelling was quite familiar. Tillich's very early "polarization" of "faith" and "doubt" has already been mentioned, see above, pp. 26–27, 66.

However, there is a difference between the first and second elements in each polarity with regard to their power of symbolizing the divine life. The elements of individualization, dynamics, and freedom represent the self or subject side of the basic ontological structure within the polarity to which they belong. The elements of participation, form, and destiny represent the world or object side of the basic ontological structure within the polarity to which they belong. Both sides are rooted in the divine life. But the first side determines the existential relationship between God and man which is the source of all symbolization.[12]

The idea of a balance between the polar elements is brought into question by man's existential situation.[13] Man is more subject than object; and therefore he symbolizes God in terms of individualization rather than participation, dynamics rather than form, freedom rather than destiny. "He sees the divine life as personal, dynamic and free."[14] Thus, as a result of this bias on the part of man, it is difficult at times to refrain from affixing higher value to the subject side of the ontological pairings and assuming a sort of hierarchy of being within each polarity.

Tillich, at various points, strives to maintain the

12. *Systematic Theology*, I, 243.
13. Tillich's explanation of the transformation of polar balance into polar tension under the conditions of finitude is not an adequate explanation of his own uneven methodological use of the principle, cf. *Systematic Theology*, I, 198–99.
14. *Systematic Theology*, I, 243.

fullness of the polar principle, but, his efforts seem to meet with less than complete success—a not unexpected eventuality in the light of the vast intellectual undertaking that is the *Systematic Theology*.[15] Something of the strain under which he labors is revealed in his discussion of the relationship of freedom and destiny. This discussion occurs in a section of the *Systematic Theology* in which the principle of polarization receives extensive application. Tillich argues that destiny is not to be defined in a deterministic fashion that would thereby place it in polar contradiction with freedom. He says that " 'destiny' . . . points to something which is going to happen to someone. . . . This makes it qualified to stand in polarity with freedom. It points not to the opposite of freedom but rather to its conditions and limits."[16]

> Destiny is not a strange power which determines what shall happen to me. It is myself as given, formed by nature, history, and myself. My destiny is the basis of my freedom; my freedom participates in shaping my destiny. . . . Only he who has freedom has a destiny. Things have no destiny because they have no freedom. . . .[17]

Despite carefully drawn definitions that are designed to assure "polar correlation" and the mutual interde-

15. See Tillich's answer to criticism about his consistency in the Kegley and Bretall volume, *The Theology of Paul Tillich*, pp. 330–31. Expression of Tillich's awareness of a distinction between the two principles is found in *Systematic Theology*, III, 319.

16. *Systematic Theology*, I, p. 185.

17. *Ibid.*

pendence of both poles, there is present in the discussions an unavoidable sense of ascent in the scale of being from "destiny" to "freedom." Tillich writes: "Our destiny is that *out of which our decisions arise;* it is the indefinitely *broad basis* of our centered selfhood. . . ."[18] The subjective bias of man threatens the integrity of the polar principle.

A somewhat more graphic example of methodological admixture is found in Tillich's discussion of the relationship of philosophy and theology and the related matter of theological method, Tillich's correlation of "existential questions and theological answers in mutual interdependence."[19] In the first instance, in treating the relationship of philosophy and theology, Tillich is concerned simply to exclude the possibility of substantive conflict between the two disciplines. He therefore defines the role and function of each in such a way that no issue can in principle be joined between them. To the degree that philosophy remains philosophy and theology remains theology opposition is ruled out. Two different levels of truth are distinguished: one governed by the cognitive attitude of detachment presupposing the subject-object cleavage (philosophy), the other governed by existential involvement and the transcendence of the subject-object dichotomy (theology). Tillich remarks: "Conflicts on the philosophical level are conflicts between two philosophers, one of whom happens to be a theologian, but they are not conflicts between theology and philosophy."[20] He also notes that conflicts occur on "the

18. *Ibid.*, p. 184. Italics mine.
19. *Ibid.*, p. 60.
20. *Ibid.*, p. 26.

theological level" when the "hidden theologian in the philosopher" takes issue with the professed theologian.

When it comes, however, to the definition of a theological method, a method designed to fulfill an apologetic task, Tillich turns to the second of the two methodological principles, that of polarization. In this instance Tillich speaks of a dependence and independence of questions and answers. The method is described as follows: "In using the method of correlation, systematic theology proceeds in the following way: it makes an analysis of the human situation out of which the existential questions arise, and it demonstrates that the symbols used in the Christian message are the answers to these questions."[21] In the light of the previous distinction between philosophy and theology, however, something of a problem arises at this point. Analysis of the human situation involves standing over-against a condition; it calls for the cognitive attitude of detachment, the distinctive mark of philosophy. Tillich declares: "The analysis of existence, including the development of the questions implicit in existence is a philosophical task, even if it is performed by a theologian. . . . As a theologian he does not tell himself what is philosophically true. As a philosopher he does not tell himself what is theologically true."[22] But having previously declared "that there is no common basis between theology and philosophy,"[23] it is difficult to see how the interdepend-

21. *Ibid.*, p. 62.
22. *Ibid.*, p. 63.
23. *Ibid.*, p. 26. This sharp distinction between philosophical and theological "levels" of truth seems also to run counter to Tillich's idea of participation of one level of being in another (see above, pp. 131–132).

ence of philosophical questions and theological answers can be consistently asserted. Yet Tillich does precisely this: "Symbolically speaking, God answers man's questions, and under the impact of God's answers man asks them. Theology formulates the questions implied in human existence, and theology formulates the answers implied in divine self-manifestation under the guidance of the questions implied in human existence."[24] Once having determined upon higher and lower levels of cognition and truth—without a "common basis"—Tillich's subsequent declaration of a reciprocal, polar relation between questions on one level and answers on another becomes problematical. That he should return to this matter of the method of correlation in the Introduction to the second volume of the *Systematic Theology* is not surprising: it is in part a response to wide criticism on the point. Perhaps it also reflects Tillich's own uneasiness about the matter.[25]

Aside from the question of complexity—and occasional confusion—in Tillich's use of two different principles for resolving ontological conflict and affirming unity of being, it is evident that both hierarchical ordering and polar interdependence have their roots in Tillich's earliest writings and that they

24. *Ibid.*, p. 61. The fact that Tillich speaks here of "theology" formulating the questions does not alter the philosophical character of the analysis of the human situation.

25. *Systematic Theology*, II, 13–16, see especially p. 14. The elaboration of the relationship of question and answer in terms of the categories "form" and "matter" does not really answer the problem. See also Robert C. Johnson's excellent discussion of Tillich's method in *Authority in Protestant Theology* (Philadelphia: Westminster Press, 1959), pp. 124–131.

play a major role in his subsequent thought. In the *Systematic Theology* they are not only determinative of methodology but contribute to systematic substance. This, however, is not all there is of the reflection of Tillich's 1912 definitions in his later thought. Certainly of no less significance than the ordering principles is the basic vision of man's encounter with the world. This too is brought to light in *Mysticism and Guilt-consciousness . . .* and then greatly expanded in the *Systematic Theology*. It is the picture of man not only as one set over-against the world, in a sense determined by it, but also as one who actively participates in shaping and molding the world.

In *Mysticism and Guilt-consciousness . . .* one will recall that in discussing the work of Kant as background for his appraisal of Schelling, Tillich especially lauded Kant's achievement in the *Critique of Judgment*. There, Tillich asserted, the principle of identity won "a surprising victory." Although observing that the nature of this victory lay hidden under Kant's intricate and complex manner of expression, Tillich nonetheless spelled out its substance in the area of aesthetic judgment as a parallel drawn between a beauty created by nature on the basis of necessity and a beauty created by man on the basis of freedom. In the later Schelling this parallelism was transformed into lower and higher levels of achievement, the higher level embracing cognitive and moral values as well as aesthetic. A footnote in the *Systematic Theology* recalls the substance of this earlier discussion of Kant (and Schelling) and points to its significance for interpreting key concepts in the *Systematic Theology*:

It is unfortunate that Kant is interpreted only as an epistemological idealist and an ethical formalist—and consequently rejected. Kant is more than this. His doctrine of the categories is a doctrine of human finitude. His doctrine of the categorical imperative is a doctrine of the unconditional element in the depth of practical reason. *His doctrine of the teleological principle in art and nature enlarges the concept of reason beyond its cognitive-technical sense toward what we have called "ontological reason."*[26]

With impressive skill and sophistication Tillich, in the *Systematic Theology*, develops the concept of reason to the point where virtually all aspects of human life, passive and active, are included within its compass. He is able to say, for example, that "classical reason"—which is also "ontological reason"—is ". . . Logos, whether it is understood in a more intuitive or in a more critical way. Its cognitive nature is one element in addition to others; it is cognitive and aesthetic, theoretical and practical, detached and passionate, subjective and objective."[27] He introduces into the representation of reason a variety of "levels" and "polarities" that at points are little short of bewildering. And he even insinuates into the discussion —as in the description of "receiving knowledge"—[28] experiential elements that can only be regarded as uniquely personal and mystical. But no more than was

26. *Systematic Theology*, I, 82. Italics mine.
27. *Ibid.*, p. 72; cf. *Systematic Theology*, II, 111: "Logos . . . unites cosmological and religious elements. It unites rational structure and creative power."
28. *Ibid.*, p. 76.

the case with Kant should Tillich's own peculiarly complex manner of expression be allowed to obscure the basic picture of man's relation to the world. Through it all, beyond method and mysticism, the outline is discernible. It is seen especially clearly in Tillich's discussion of "subjective reason." As man's subjectivity determined the symbolization of being-itself, so also it fixes the basic meaning of "ontological reason."

> Subjective reason is the structure of the mind which enables it to grasp and to shape reality on the basis of a corresponding structure of reality (in whatever way this correspondence may be explained). The description of "grasping" and "shaping" in this definition is based on the fact that subjective reason always is actualized in an individual self which is related to its environment and to its world in terms of reception and reaction. The mind receives and reacts. In receiving reasonably the mind grasps its world; in reacting reasonably, the mind shapes its world. "Grasping," in this context, has the connotation of penetrating into the depth, into the essential nature of a thing or an event, of understanding and expressing it. "Shaping," in this context, has the connotation of transforming a given material into a Gestalt, a living structure which has the power of being.[29]

The introduction of the term "Gestalt" into the concluding sentence of the description has the effect,

29. *Ibid.*, p. 76.

for those unfamiliar with Tillich's German writings, of casting something of a pall over the discussion. Rather than providing clarification its effect is to obfuscate, for "Gestalt" is a word or concept which Tillich fails to define in this context. In other places it is used sometimes in relation to conceptualization[30] and sometimes in relation to things.[31] Its basic meaning however is the idea of "wholeness."[32] A "gestalt" represents an ordering of multiplicity, whether of ideas or of objects. It is the establishment of a meaningful and useful coherence that can, in its coherence and "rightness," react upon the mind of man. Thus Tillich can say: "Man is able to create a world beyond the given world; he creates the technical and the spiritual realms."[33] And further:

> [Man's] creativity breaks through the biological realm to which he belongs and establishes new realms never attainable on a non-human level. Man is able to create a new world of technical tools and a world of cultural forms. In both cases something new comes into being through man's grasping and shaping activity. Man uses the material given by nature to create technical forms which transcend nature, and he creates cultural forms which have validity and meaning. Living in these forms, he transforms himself, while originating them. He is not only a tool for their creation; he is at the same time their bearer and the

30. *S.T.* II, 103–6.
31. *S.T.* III, 259.
32. *S.T.* III, 33.
33. *Systematic Theology*, I, 180.

result of their transforming effect upon him. His self-transcendence in this direction is indefinite. . . .[34]

In the designation of man's "grasping" and "shaping" function, we are actually brought to the heart of Tillich's thought, both early and late. Tillich's ontological concerns—the separation of subject and object, the one and the many, freedom and destiny—find final resolution within a "creative process" rooted in an eternal "ground and power of being" inexhaustible in potentiality. For man to create is for man to transcend the subject-object cleavage through a reordering of objects and ideas into new patterns of meaning—and this on the basis of freedom. To create is to introduce unities within previously existing multiplicities. As Tillich states it: "Every aesthetic image or cognitive concept is . . . a structured whole. Ideally, the mind drives toward an image that embraces all images and a concept that contains all concepts, but in reality the universe never appears in a direct vision —it only shines through particular images and concepts."[35] Man in his finitude cannot create a final synthesis, he cannot transcend absolutely the subject-object and the one-many dichotomies, but in his finite creations the creative ground of all being can be manifested.

This picture of man's twofold relation to the world, sustained by the "ground and power of being," is absolutely indispensable to an understanding of Tillich's

34. *Systematic Theology*, I, 181–82; cf. also *Systematic Theology*, III, 57–68.
35. *Systematic Theology*, III, 62.

work. Its fundamental importance is attested by its ramifications throughout the system. From this key point access is had to virtually all avenues of Tillich's thought. Elaboration of man's grasping and shaping functions leads naturally into such basic matters as the points of similarity and difference between God and man, the root meaning of Tillich's distinction between essence and existence, and the definition of faith as "ultimate concern." Illustrations of these points follows, but first a source of possible major misunderstanding must be treated.

Immediately after the definitive description of the grasping and shaping functions,[36] Tillich offers statement of the relationship of the two functions to each other. The original, relatively clear-cut differentiation is at once clouded by the suggestion of a balanced, polar interdependence:

> The division between the grasping and shaping character of reason is not exclusive. In every act of reasonable reception an act of shaping is involved, and in every act of reasonable reaction an act of grasping is involved. We transform reality according to the way we see it and we see reality according to the way we transform it. Grasping and shaping the world are interdependent.[37]

However impressive the application of the polar principle may appear to be at this point, however convincing its yield, one errs in supposing that Tillich

36. See above, p. 142.
37. *Systematic Theology,* I, 76.

actually intends a full-standing balance and interdependence of the "grasping" and "shaping" functions. Tillich's utilization of the principle of polarization here is in fact misleading, for the main thrust of his thought is the subordination of the noetic function to the creative. The former is, as it were, taken up into the latter. Therefore any assumption of an equal weighting of grasping and shaping activities distorts the picture and undercuts important arguments at other points. A balanced polarity of the two functions, for example, works against Tillich's own earlier definition of the relationship of philosophy (synonymous with "grasping") and theology (synonymous with "shaping").[38] It also threatens the viability of Tillich's concept of "objective reason."[39] That man shapes reality on the basis of how he *previously* grasped it is clear. And that man in shaping reality has an effect upon how reality is *later* grasped is also clear. But that man shapes reality *as* he grasps it is a highly problematical proposition in terms of the logic of the system. If Tillich at this point actually proposes the simultaneity and equivalence of the grasping and shaping functions, rather than a sequential and inclusive relationship (and it is not clear from the passage that he does), then this proposal can only be regarded as a foreign body within the system.

As a matter of fact Tillich's substantive subordination of the noetic to the creative function is found

38. *Systematic Theology*, I, 18–28. The identification of theology with the "shaping" function follows; see below pp. 154–156.
39. Cf. *Systematic Theology*, I, 77–79.

146

throughout the *Systematic Theology* (and his earlier thought) in his consistent accent upon man's *creative* affinity with God. It is not in "knowing," but rather in "doing," in dynamically altering reality, that man most surely expresses his kinship with God. This is certainly the meaning of a passage such as the following:

> Creation is the creation of finite freedom; it is the creation of life with its greatness and its danger. God lives, and his life is creative. If God is creative in himself, he cannot create the dead, the object which is merely object. He must create that which unites subjectivity and objectivity—life, that which includes freedom and with it the dangers of freedom.[40]

Many similar statements of man's participation in God's creative power are found throughout the three volumes of the *Systematic Theology*, but this cannot be said for statements linking human and divine knowledge. Clearly, for Tillich, freedom and will represent the climactic expression of life. The point is confirmed by Tillich himself when, after asserting the polar interdependence of "knowing" and "doing," he declares: "Only in the active realization of the true does truth become manifest."[41] A concluding positive estimate of the philosophical significance of Karl Marx removes all doubt of the paramountcy of doing over knowing. A dynamic, hierarchical ordering rather

40. *Ibid.*, p. 269.
41. *Ibid.*, p. 76.

147

than polarization represents more faithfully Tillich's true intent in regard to the relationship of man's grasping and shaping functions.

Beyond question stress upon man's creative capacity stands as the commanding feature of Tillich's thought, both early and late. Knowing the truth must pass over into doing the truth: on this assumption the kairos doctrine and Religious Socialism were founded. On this assumption also the *Systematic Theology* builds. As suggested, creative power represents the unbreakable bond between God and man. By means of it man transcends the split of subject-object, one-many. By means of it he realizes his freedom and builds a world. He does so, however, always within limits. And Tillich does not hesitate to say this also. Affinity between God and man in creative power does not exclude noting a difference between God's creativity and man's:

> If creativity means "to bring the new into being," man is creative in every direction—with respect to himself and his world, with respect to being and with respect to meaning. However, if creativity means "to bring into being that which had no being," then divine and human creativity differ sharply. Man creates new syntheses out of given material. This creation really is transformation. God creates the material out of which the new syntheses can be developed. God creates man, he gives man the power of transforming himself and his world. Man can transform only what is given to him. God is primarily and essen-

148

tially creative; man is secondarily and existentially creative.[42]

In short, God is infinitely creative, man is finitely so.[43]

In drawing the difference between divine and human creativity, the early study of Schelling once more aids Tillich in his conceptualization. As Schelling had spoken of God as "Synthesis," the ground of all being, the ultimate basis of the "coincidence of opposites," so also he spoke of God's infinite, initiatory power. God, Schelling said, ". . . separates himself from himself, sets himself against himself," in order "to lead darkness into light."[44] If the first image of God, that of "synthesis," conveys the idea of containment, the second projects a sense of God's unlimited vitality, expressiveness, creativity.[45] The second image as well as the first is preserved in Tillich's thought: "The divine life is creative, actualizing itself in inexhaustible abundance. The divine life and the divine creativity are not different. God is creative because he is God."[46] Lest God's creativity be interpreted as somehow motivated by deficiency or want, Tillich declares: "His aseity implies that everything which he is he is through himself. He eternally

42. *Ibid.*, p. 256.
43. Cf. *ibid.*, pp. 235–237.
44. See above, p. 120.
45. Whether Tillich achieves a complete and fully satisfying synthesis of these concepts of God is really a matter for each one to decide for himself. Cf. *Systematic Theology*, I, 247–48, 249; *Systematic Theology*, III, 401–02.
46. *Systematic Theology*, I, 252; cf. *Systematic Theology*, II, 147.

'creates himself,' a paradoxical phrase which states God's freedom . . . Creation [is not] contingent. It does not 'happen' to God, for it is identical with his life. Creation is not only God's freedom but also his destiny."[47]

Obviously the fullness of God's infinite creativity is beyond the mind of man to probe. Necessarily Tillich must speak of mystery: "The creative process of the divine life precedes the differentiation between essences and existents. . . . The mystery of being beyond essence and existence is hidden in the mystery of the divine life."[48] But no such ultimate limit restricts examination of man's creativity. Whereas God is beyond essence and existence, man's creativity arises in the midst of—one really must say, "as a result of"—the separation of essence and existence.

At this point it is advisable to guard against any deep involvement in Tillich's equation of divine creation and "the fall," an aspect of the analysis of the separation of essence and existence. It represents a worried phase of Tillich's thought.[49] He himself describes it as "the most difficult and the most dialectical point in the doctrine of creation," as "the most mys-

47. *Systematic Theology*, I, 252; cf. *Systematic Theology*, I, 263–64.

48. *Systematic Theology*, I, 255.

49. Many theologians have been critical of Tillich's identification of "creation" and "fall"; see especially Reinhold Niebuhr's criticism in Kegley and Bretall, *op. cit.*, pp. 219–225. For early discussion of the "fall" by Tillich, see his account of the classical concept of the "fall of the world of ideas" and Schelling's adaptation of it: *Gesammette Werke*, I, 66–67.

terious point in human experience."[50] He speaks of
man's being both "inside" and "outside" the process of
the divine life. "Man," Tillich declares, "has left the
[divine ground] in order to 'stand upon' himself, to
actualize what he essentially is, in order to be finite
freedom."[51] But then he also says, "Man [exists], and
his existence is different from his essence."[52] From
such statements it appears that man, in realizing what
he essentially is (i.e. finite freedom), experiences a
separation from essence—a "dialectical" thought to
say the least.[53] In the face of such ambiguity, one
must seek elsewhere the substance of what Tillich has
to say about the separation of essence and existence.[54]
And what he *does* have to say on the subject is contained in a generalized discussion of essence which
precedes his account of "the fall." There Tillich notes
a duality of meaning in the use of the term "essence."
He identifies an "empirical" and "valuating sense" of
the word:

> Essence as the nature of a thing, or as the qual-
> ity in which a thing participates, or as a univer-

50. *Systematic Theology*, I, 255.
51. *Ibid.*
52. *Ibid.*
53. A second statement of the matter runs as follows: "The
goodness of man's created nature is that he is given the
possibility and necessity of actualizing himself and of becoming independent by his self-actualization, in spite of the
estrangement unavoidably connected with it." (*Systematic
Theology*, I, 259.)
54. Tillich himself suggests that he is driven to an equation
of "creation" and "fall" by other more basic considerations,
cf. *Systematic Theology*, II, 43–44.

sal, has one character. Essence as that from which being has "fallen," the true undistorted nature of things, has another character. In the second case essence is the basis of value judgments, while in the first case essence is a logical ideal to be reached by abstraction or intuition without the interference of valuations. . . . Essence as that which makes a thing *what* it is (*ousia*) has a purely logical character; essence as that which appears in an imperfect and distorted way in a thing carries the stamp of value.[55]

Although in this context Tillich ascribes something of a negative character to the "valuating sense" of essence—he speaks of essence as "judging" existence and "standing against" it "as commanding law"[56]—its significance is principally viewed in positive terms. In volume two of the *Systematic Theology* Tillich writes: "Man is free, in so far as he can receive unconditional moral and logical imperatives which indicate that he can transcend the conditions which determine every finite being."[57] And again, "The essential or potential in man and his world is the source from which the norms for life in the dimension of spirit are derived."[58] These "norms for life" in turn inspire the

55. *Systematic Theology* I, 202–3. In these few sentences it is clear that we have a sort of metaphysical basis for the "grasping" and "shaping" functions in man.

56. *Ibid.*, p. 203.

57. *Systematic Theology*, II, 31; cf. *Systematic Theology*, I, 246. Tillich sees in the law of Judaism expression of man's essential nature; cf. *Systematic Theology*, II, 81.

58. *Systematic Theology*, III, 29; cf. *Systematic Theology*, III, 164: ". . . Everywhere, the essential is one of the determining powers."

creative will of man. They are "ambiguously" present in the movement of life and call for courage and risk on man's part:

> There is no straight and certain way to the norms of action in the dimension of spirit. The sphere of the potential is partly visible, partly hidden. Therefore, the application of a norm to a concrete situation in the realm of the spirit, is a venture and a risk. It requires courage and acceptance of the possibility of failure. The daring character of life in its creative functions holds true also in the dimension of spirit, in morality, culture, and religion.[59]

The separation of essence from existence, the presence within existence of a "valuating sense" of essence, a sense of the "ought-to-be" and the "not-yet," characterizes the human situation. Living in the midst of the separation, man finds in it purpose and meaning for life.[60]

59. *Systematic Theology*, III, 29–30.
60. As a very important aspect of this idea of the "valuating sense" of essence one must note that Tillich seeks to avoid a kind of classical platonism. He insists that eternity is not "a return to what a thing essentially is" (*Systematic Theology*, III, 400), but rather . . . that essence is "*creatively enriched in existence*" (*Systematic Theology*, III, 402). In the third volume of the *Systematic Theology* he uses the term "essentialization" to express this enrichment of value in existence (cf. *Ibid.*, 400–402). In effect Tillich proposes a concept of dynamic value and thereby further helps to establish the necessity of a "metaphysics of history" (cf. *Systematic Theology*, III, 302–305). This is not really a new idea for Tillich; Religious Socialism was early buttressed by the idea of "dynamic truth."

Significantly, as one pursues analysis of the source of the creative impulse in man, one catches a glimpse of its potential universal incidence. This is a matter of no small consequence to Tillich. Since his concept of man's shaping function is an outgrowth of the aesthetic philosophy of Kant and Schelling, he is vulnerable to the charge that the aesthetic point of origin represents too narrow a base on which to build a comprehensive anthropology (and theology).[61] A sense of creative achievement is far from being a universal human experience. Tillich is sensitive to the point: he sees the need for gathering all men into the fold of creative endeavor. Thus, while recognizing the fact that not everyone is a cultural innovator, he nevertheless insists that all men share a creative role by virtue of their participation in culture. "A person who participates in a culture's movement, growth, and possible destruction is culturally creative. In this sense, every human being is culturally creative, simply by virtue of speaking and using tools."[62] More tellingly Tillich argues that all men share the same desire and drive that motivates the artist, an awareness of meaning and values and a longing to actualize these values. To Til-

61. Tillich himself had earlier deplored a limitation of the religious meaning of life to man's moral sense; see above p. 119. Cf. also Tillich, "Albrecht Ritschl: Zu seinem hundertsten Geburtstag," *Theologische Blätter*, I, No. 3 (March 1922), 52. The same sort of concern is mirrored in Tillich's discussion of "myth" and "cult" and the "depth of reason," *Systematic Theology*, I, 79–81.

62. *Systematic Theology*, III, 68. Participation in the destruction of a culture can be viewed as creative because it is generally inspired by a desire for new possibilities of life. Tillich has in mind the protest against decaying cultural forms, a feature of the Protestant principle.

lich's mind affirmation of the self is ultimately inseparable from the whole realm of meanings and values
which is culture. Without value, without meaning,
there can be no future, no purpose, no goal for human
life. In the final analysis it is meaning and value which
beckon life, which define purposes and instill in man
the power "to be."

With this broadened interpretation of man's "shaping" function, one descries what lies behind Tillich's
differentiation of philosophy and theology. "Philosophy deals with the structure of being in itself."[63]
But "theology deals with *the meaning of being for
us*."[64] Theology is involvement with value, it is pas-
sion, it is "ultimate concern." Examination of Tillich's
"two formal critera of theology"[65] helps chart the universal basis of "religion." Amidst all the manifold
concerns and purposes of men, there must be for
every man an ultimate concern, a value sought, in part
realized, that determines his "being or not being." All
men who choose to live, who address themselves to to-
morrow, are religious and theological in this degree.[66]
Though himself convinced that being-itself, the
ground and power of being, God, should be the final,
conscious focus of man's ultimate concern,[67] Tillich,
in his definition of faith, allows for less, because he
sees in being-itself an active power upholding all
things and transcendently directing them—in their

63. *Systematic Theology*, I, 22.
64. *Ibid.*, Italics mine.
65. *Ibid.*, 11–15.
66. Cf. *Systematic Theology*, I, 24–25.
67. Cf. *Ibid.*, 273.

155

freedom—to an ultimate end. God, Tillich declares, is no spectator:

> . . . God's directing creativity always creates through the freedom of man and through the spontaneity and structural wholeness of all creatures. Providence works . . . through the conditions of individual, social, and universal existence, through finitude, nonbeing, and anxiety, through the interdependence of all finite things, through their resistance against the divine activity and through the destructive consequences of this resistance. All existential conditions are included in God's directing creativity.[68]

To conclude, each man, creatively pursuing his own goals and purposes, is contained within and contributes to God's final purpose of life.

If, in the light of all this, one asks what is the place and meaning of Christ, the answer must come that his place and meaning are essentially determined by the aprioristic anthropology, the "grasping-shaping" definition of man.

It is the case, in the "Introduction" of the *Systematic Theology*, that in speaking of the theological circle[69]—and what later becomes a theological ellipse—[70] Tillich recognizes a sort of ultimate commitment by the Christian theologian, a commitment to the con-

68. *Ibid.*, 266. For an equivalent, early statement of this view of providence, see Tillich's quotation of Schelling, *Mystik und Schuldbewusstsein . . .*, *Gesammelte Werke*, I, 55.
69. *Ibid.*, 8–11.
70. *Systematic Theology*, II, 14–15.

crete image of Jesus as the Christ that qualifies the more general "mystical a priori" characteristic of philosophers of religion.[71] Tillich says of the Christian theologian, for example, that he "claims the universal validity of the Christian message in spite of its concrete and special character. He does not justify this claim by abstracting from the concreteness of the message but by stressing its unrepeatable uniqueness. He enters the theological circle with a concrete commitment. He enters it as a member of the Christian church. . . ."[72] Here Tillich sets out the possibility of subordinating all philosophical schema, his own ontologically-oriented anthropology included, to commitment to Christ;[73] and one should not lightly dismiss this transposition of the theological function into the frame of reference of the Church. But in terms of all that follows in the *Systematic Theology*, it must be said that the content of the meaning of Christ is in major part determined by "outside" philosophical considerations.[74] In the final analysis Tillich's Christology chiefly feeds back into that creative process that is envisioned as the fulfillment of human potentiality, the answer to traditional ontological questionings.

To forward this estimate it is not necessary to enter upon an exhaustive analysis of Tillich's Christology. A sketch of its highlights will suffice. The point

71. *Systematic Theology*, I, 9.
72. *Ibid.*, 10.
73. On this point—and in regard to Tillich himself—one is prompted to recall Tillich's 1934 stand with Barth against Hirsch, in spite of greater philosophical affinity with the latter; see above, pp. 79–80.
74. Cf. R. C. Johnson, *op. cit.*, 134–38. Johnson's analysis of Tillich's method is very perceptive on this point.

of beginning is Tillich's analysis of the human malaise:

All creaturely existence, Tillich declares, draws upon a power of being that has its origin in being-itself. It is in the power of being-itself that the creature is able "to resist nonbeing."[75] But, in man, resistance against nonbeing is also joined with a "resistance against the ground of being," a possibility inherent in finite freedom. Confronted in life with the inevitability of transitoriness and death, yet aware of infinite being, man becomes "anxious."[76] He attempts to secure his own life independent of God and in defiance of Him: he seeks to elevate himself above the limits of finitude. In this, man sins.[77] He . . . "identifies his cultural creativity with divine creativity. He attributes infinite significance to his finite cultural creations making idols of them, elevating them into matters of ultimate concern."[78] The end result is that man suffers a disruption of self-hood[79] beyond his own powers to heal.[80]

Principally Tillich argues that for man there is an "essential finitude" marked by limitation in time and

75. *Systematic Theology*, I, 261.
76. *Ibid.*, 189–91.
77. *Systematic Theology*, II, 46, 50–51.
78. *Ibid.*, 51. Cf. Tillich's concept of the demonic, *Systematic Theology*, I, 134; *Systematic Theology*, II, 73; *Systematic Theology*, III, 344.
79. *Systematic Theology*, II, 60–62, 62–66.
80. *Ibid.*, 78–9. This strong statement of the need for grace seems to represent a new accent in Tillich's thought. It is clear from the subsequent analysis, however, that this assertion of the need for grace does not involve revision of Tillich's basic Christology, derived fundamentally from Schelling.

space, death, suffering, and solitude.[81] These aspects of finitude, though they create anxiety and insecurity, do *not* necessitate sin. They do *not* demand a severance of man's tie with being-itself. As a matter of fact, in "essential finitude" being-itself provides ". . . an ultimate security or certainty which does not cancel out the preliminary insecurities and uncertainties of finitude. . . . Rather it takes them into itself with the courage to accept one's finitude."[82] Actually, however, every man sins. Every man turns away from the ultimate security of being-itself, to establish his own "security," a false security that cannot and does not endure. The universality of this pattern forces one to speak of an "existential finitude," a distortion of "essential finitude," an "estrangement" of man from God, for which man stands responsible but about which he can do nothing. His helplessness, in part at least, is traceable to the fact that he is unaware of his sinful condition.[83]

The Christological "answer" to "existential finitude" and "estrangement" is, of course, the assertion that in Jesus as the Christ "essential finitude," or the "New Being," or "essential God-Manhood" is actualized. The image of Christ, Tillich declares, "does not represent man to God but shows what God wants man to be. He represents to those who live under the conditions of existence what man essentially is and therefore ought to be under these conditions."[84] Tillich re-

81. *Systematic Theology*, II, 66–75, especially p. 73.
82. *Ibid.*, 73.
83. *Systematic Theology*, II, 92. Note the proper sense of "paradox."
84. *Systematic Theology*, II, 93; cf. *Ibid.*, 118–119.

jects the idea that "Jesus as the Christ" is "a personal unity of a divine and a human nature" and offers as an alternative the declaration that "in Jesus as the Christ the eternal unity of God and man has become historical reality."[85] That which is potential in every man, the unity between God and man (what one might also call "true humanity"), is actualized in Jesus as the Christ. Tillich sums it up in the following manner:

> The paradox of the Christian message is not that essential humanity includes the union of God and man. *This belongs to the dialectics of the infinite and the finite.* The paradox of the Christian message is that in *one* personal life essential manhood has appeared under the conditions of existence without being conquered by them.[86]

In development of this Christology of "true humanity" Tillich shows how Jesus as the Christ, as represented in the Synoptic Gospels, experienced all the anxieties of finitude[87] without yielding to the temptations of self-exaltation or concupiscence. To the end, in the power of the New Being, Jesus accepted his finitude. This was manifested not alone in the Cross, but in Jesus' *continual* willingness to sacri-

85. *Ibid.*, 148.

86. *Ibid.*, 94. I have italicized the second sentence because it indicates the philosophical character of the question of the union of God and man. Quite apart from the revelation of the Christ in Jesus a philosophical a priori (the coincidence of opposites) assures a unity of God and man. Cf. *Systematic Theology*, II, 148; *Gesammelte Werke*, I, 22–23.

87. *Systematic Theology*, II, 125–135.

fice himself by pointing beyond himself to God. In this life of sacrifice, Jesus fulfilled the role of the Christ; he fulfilled the role of bearer of the New Being.[88] Tillich, in treating the question of "final revelation," states the sum of it:

> He who is the bearer of the final revelation must surrender his finitude—not only his life but also his finite power and knowledge and perfection. In doing so, he affirms that he is the bearer of final revelation. . . . He becomes completely transparent to the mystery he reveals.[89] This means that in following him we are liberated from the authority of everything finite in him, from his special traditions, from his individual piety, from his rather conditioned world view, from any legalistic understanding of his ethics. Only as the crucified is he "grace and truth" and not law.[90]

Although at times Schelling seems to have been more willing than Tillich to speak of "incarnation"

88. *Ibid.*, 123. For a discussion of the sense in which the "New Being" is "new," see *Systematic Theology*, II, 119. The point is important because Tillich is here again confronted with the "necessity" of denying that "the end is the beginning" (see above, p. 153 n. 60); it is the equivalent of "essence being enriched in existence." The problem of "Adam" and "dreaming innocence" also bear upon the discussion; cf. *Systematic Theology*, II, 32–34.
89. *Systematic Theology*, I, 133.
90. *Ibid.*, p. 134. Tavard is certainly right in closely joining Tillich's Christology and statement of the Protestant principle; Tavard, *op. cit.*, pp. 101–103.

in the traditional sense,[91] it is clear that the content of Schelling's Christology was similarly determined by the idea of self-sacrifice. In *Mysticism and Guilt-consciousness* . . . Tillich quotes Schelling on the subject of Christ's glory: "This glory, however, which he could have independent of the Father, the Son scorns, and in this fact he is Christ. This is the fundamental idea of Christianity."[92] Christ's sacrifice, for both Schelling and Tillich, is a repudiation of every form of self-elevation. In Tillich, it is pressed to the point of specifically excluding a second idea of sacrifice, that of "substitutionary sacrifice," or a dying "on behalf of" others.[93] Tillich asserts that the function of Christ is to *manifest* the New Being, to show forth the essential humanity that is potential in every man. As a result, the uniqueness of the event "Jesus as the Christ" gives way to its potential duplication in every man.[94] It yields to a universal potentiality for sacrifice that is paradoxically affirmed as every man's hope of salvation and healing. In sacrificing all claims to absoluteness, for himself *and his cultural creations,* man

91. Cf. *Mystik und Schuldewusstsein* . . . , *Gesammelte Werke* I, 95–7. Cf. *Systematic Theology*, II, pp. 94–5, 148–50.
92. *Gesammelte Werke* I, 108. Cf. *Ibid.,* 97.
93. *Systematic Theology*, II, 173–76; especially 176.
94. Cf. *Systematic Theology*, II, 129–30 (N.B., the third step in the treatment of Jesus' temptations). Cf. *Systematic Theology*, II, 116: "Of course, in terms of historical documentation we do know many people better than Jesus. But in terms of personal participation in his being, we do not know anyone better because his being is the New Being which is universally valid for every human being." Cf. also *Systematic Theology*, II, 166–67, 179–80; *Systematic Theology*, III, 140, 146–47.

162

fulfills his being as finite freedom and thus assures—
not incidentally—continuation of the creative process. Tillich remarks: "Genuine sacrifice fulfills rather
than annihilates him who makes the sacrifice,"[95]—
the meaning of which is conveyed in another passage:

> Not all the creative possibilities of a person,
> or all the creative possibilites of the human race,
> have been or will be actualized. The Spiritual
> Presence does not change that situation—for
> although the finite can participate in the infinite,
> it cannot become infinite—but the Spirit can
> create an acceptance of man's and mankind's
> finitude, and in so doing can give a new meaning
> to the sacrifice of potentialities.[96]

By "sacrificing" claim to fulfillment of *all* of one's
potentialities, the fulfillment of one, or a few, is possible. It is here that one is called upon to "accept
acceptance," to accept the reality of one's finitude
and repent the sinfulness of self-exaltation and to do
this within the compass of being-itself.[97] One is called
to realize that in the end one cannot save oneself, that
in the end all of one's powers and potentialities, all of
one's creative achievements, are also gifts received. In
the image of Jesus as the Christ, Tillich declares, the
divine Spirit "shows the sacrifice of all human potentialities for the sake of the one which man himself cannot actualize, the uninterrupted unity with God. *But
the image also shows that this sacrifice is indirectly*

95. *Systematic Theology*, III, 392.
96. *Ibid.*, 271.
97. *Systematic Theology*, II, 178—179.

*creative in all directions of truth, expressiveness, humanity, justice. . . .*"[98]

In short once one grasps—or rather is grasped by —[99] the infinite acceptance of finite life, the future is opened to confident, joyful action. The necessity of deciding between alternatives is positively affirmed. Although to decide means also to exclude other possibilities of good, decisions are freely made in awareness that the only "right decisions" are those that sacrifice their claim to being right decisions.

> . . . There *are* decisions which are rooted in love, which by resigning the absolute do not fall into the relative. They are not exposed to the revenge of the excluded possibilities because they were and still are open for them. No decision can be annihilated; no action can be undone. But love gives meaning even to those decisions and actions which prove to be failures. The failures of love do not lead to resignation but to new decisions beyond absolutism and relativism.[100]

The burden and direction of Tillich's Christology is ultimately a purging and cleansing of man's activi-

98. *Systematic*, III, 271. Italics mine.

99. The sense of being "grasped by" a meaning or value represents the Nietzschean influence upon Tillich and is basic to Tillich's thought. It expresses the reality of a supra-individualistic quality of life, the presence of transcendence within history. The category which Tillich usually uses to express this meaning is "ecstasy" or "ecstatic reason." Cf. *Systematic Theology*, I, 111–15. 117. It found early expression in Tillich's thought; cf. *Gesammelte Werke*, I, 198–200, 289, 314–15, 335–37, 354.

100. *Systematic Theology*, I, 153.

ties in anticipation of an ultimate coalescence of human and divine creativity, a final union of God and man in act.

> . . . Eternal Life is the end of culture. Culture was defined as the self-creativity of life under the dimension of the spirit, and it was divided into *theoria*, in which reality is received, and *praxis*, in which reality is shaped. . . . In Eternal Life there is no truth which is not also "done." . . . There is no aesthetic expression which is not also a reality. Beyond this, culture as spiritual creativity becomes, at the same time, Spiritual creativity. The human spirit's creativity in Eternal Life is revelation by the divine Spirit. . . . Man's creativity and divine self-manifestation are one in the fulfilled Kingdom of God.[101]

This is the reality and promise of the New Being in Jesus as the Christ. It sets man's creativity in the light of a universal grace of God and points to an ultimate dynamic identity.

\*     \*     \*

In appraising over-all the course of Tillich's thought, in assessing the relation of the early thought to the later, one cannot but confirm Tillich's own judgment that a "few great and lasting things" were decisive for his mind. On this there can be no question. Over the years and in face of the events through which he lived, the consistency of his concerns is little short of remarkable. Never did he leave behind those dichotomies of subject-object, one-many, freedom-destiny

101. *Systematic Theology*, III, 403.

that so early occupied his mind. Never did he leave behind the vision of man's advance beyond these dichotomies, their temporary transcendence in man's various artistic and ethical achievements. In the creative act, when man, in freedom, accomplishes a transfer of meaning from subject (and the realm of Spirit) to object, or when a previously existing multiplicity is given order and unity in some new form (*Gestalt*), there and then the cleavage between subject and object, the one and the many, is overcome. There "destiny" is caught up in freedom, and Spirit is made manifest. Such creativity is man's reflection, within the limits of finitude, of a divine life, infinitely creative, a divine life that underlies the spiritual process of history and is not exhausted in any particular creation or cultural synthesis. The Unconditional, or Being-Itself, "shines through" with special brilliance, as it were, during periods of "theonomy"; but then it continues its course, calling man to move with it. Sin and its concomitant, guilt, occur when man attempts to deny the divine life, and the movement of history, when man sets himself at the center of the world and absolutizes his own powers and cultural creations. Jesus, as the Christ, exposes the depth of sin (the ought-not-to-be) in his own self-sacrifice and simultaneously points man to the ongoing work of Spirit (the ought-to-be) in history. Here is the nub of Tillich's thought, both early and late. Herein lies the basis for Tillich's use of Marxian categories in Religious Socialism, his identification of the proletariat as the bearer of the new spiritual forces emerging in history. Herein lies the basis also for Tillich's later abandonment of the corporate-historical emphasis in favor of the more adaptable categories of "New Being," "ultimate concern," and "the courage to be." In short, what has been argued in these last two chapters is that the basic ideational side of Tillich's life is not adequately treated—or understood—if explanation is not given of this body of ideas that made possible both Religious Socialism and the *Systematic Theology*—ideas spelled out in Tillich's pre-World War I study of Schelling, *Mysticism and Guilt-consciousness* . . .

It is not unlikely that this thesis will encounter some protest from other Tillich interpreters who somehow imagine that World War I represented a more radical break in Tillich's thought than in fact it was. To be sure, some of Tillich's autobiographical statements suggest a radical reappraisal of thought arising out of the World War I experience; for example, Tillich's assertion that "the World War in my own experience was the catastrophe of idealistic thinking in general. Even Schelling's philosophy was drawn into the catastrophe."[102] But at another place Tillich also declared:

> Another prelude to the things to come occurred in the period between my student years and the beginning of the First World War. It was the encounter with Schelling's second period, especially with his so-called "Positive Philosophy." Here lies the philosophically decisive break with Hegel, and the beginning of that which today is called Existentialism. I was ready for it when it appeared in full strength after the First World War. . . .[103]

102. *Interpretation of History*, p. 35.
103. Kegley and Bretall, p. 11.

167

Obviously one is confronted here with a less than clear picture of the impact of World War I upon Tillich's thought. Certainly the Marxian, anti-bourgeois theme represents an outgrowth of the war situation, so too the Nietzschean motif of transcendent spirit, the repudiation of Hegelian pan-logism.[104] But this entailed really only a revision of the Schellingian philosophy of history. Here, it seems, one must guard against supposing that because World War I represented a radical break in the thought of Karl Barth and other "neo-orthodox" thinkers, this must have been true also for Tillich. Let me assert that this was simply not the case. And, as in the matter of Tillich's statement about the beginning of his work on the *Systematic Theology*, a judgment on this can be made only against the background of his actual writings.

In this connection note must be taken of an assertion by Wilhelm Pauck that Tillich was most precise in the recall of situations and conditions surrounding new insights that came to him in the course of his life.[105] This, coming as a personal reminiscence of Pauck, is interesting and no doubt should be given consideration by those who set themselves the task of outlining the development of Tillich's thought. But a more basic and safer premise on which to proceed in this matter is Tillich's own admission, in the preface to *The Protestant Era:* "It sometimes strikes me (and this is probably a very common experience),

104. Cf. Tillich, "Ueber die Idee einer Theologie der Kultur," *Religionsphilosophie der Kultur*, (Berlin: Reuther & Reichard, 1919), p. 31.
105. Wilhelm Pauck, "Paul Tillich: 1886–1965," *Theology Today*, XXIII, No. 1 (April, 1966), 4.

when I read some of my earliest writings, how much of what I believed to be a recent achievement is already explicitly or at least implicitly contained in them."[106]

What has been argued in these pages is that the writings before World War I—really the one piece *Mysticism and Guilt-consciousness* . . .—constitute the indispensable guide to determining the structure of Tillich's thought. Fichte, Kant, Hegel, Schleiermacher represent thinkers whom Tillich knew intimately before World War I. Through his pre-war studies of Schelling he was also introduced to Boehme and Baader. This background lies behind and informs the argument of *Mysticism and Guilt-consciousness.* . . . Marx and Nietzsche—and also Troeltsch—represent the post-World War I influences upon Tillich, but these latter thinkers, it should be clear, did not force a recasting of the basic dynamic ontology that Tillich outlined in the 1912 work.

There may be some Tillich interpreters who will assert that there are major innovations in point of view in some of Tillich's larger writings of the 1920's, *The System of the Sciences* . . . , "Philosophy of Religion," or *Religious Realization*. This may only represent a quarrel over the word "major," but I have not found this to be the case. Perhaps those who incline to the other view will still have something to say on the point.

106. *The Protestant Era*, pp. x–xi.

# VI

## "ARTIST'S" POSTSCRIPT

What then is to be said of this theological portrait? The various elements that comprise it bear a certain completeness in their separate parts as well as sharing a relationship to each other. Each encounter and analysis adds depth to our picture, another dimension to our understanding of Tillich's thought. Yet, as a theological portrait, the whole needs interpretation if it is to fulfill its purpose of supplying an overview of Tillich and his work. The reader can, of course, provide his own interpretation and is urged to do so. But he is also entitled, I think, to know something more of the mind of the present writer in constructing this picture and in viewing it now at its completion.

\*　　\*　　\*

As originally suggested, theological portraiture is designed to illumine the bond of life and thought, to

170

explore what I have termed the "life quality" of Tillich's thought. Tillich himself insisted on this tie of life and thought and at times was boldly explicit about the existential bases of his thinking. Indeed, his various autobiographical reflections are so unique in this regard that they elicit speculation about Tillich's purpose in offering them. These "intellectual confessions" make problematical, I think, any interpretative approach to Tillich's thought that leaves out of analysis the man himself and certain formative experiences and concerns that were his.

The necessity of taking such account of the human equation is not a happy eventuality. It runs counter to the niceties of academic custom and at points forces consideration of the *argumentum ad hominem.* But is not this an implication of the way in which Tillich viewed his own life and thought? As I read his autobiographical reflections I am impressed with Tillich's sense of the providential in his life, a not uncommon feature of the life of faith. Seemingly it led him to probe the meaning of varied life experiences and allowed him to find large meanings in what others might regard as small events. Generally it was the case that Tillich saw his life in large terms. His 1936 autobiographical sketch, "On the Boundary,"[1] bears witness to this fact. But with it all Tillich maintained proportion. He understood the vagaries of the self and of history. And in the end he soberly committed the judgment about his "system," his great effort at reconciling religion and culture, theology and philosophy, to the church.[2]

1. *Interpretation of History*, pp. 3–73.
2. *Systematic Theology*, I, 48–9.

When viewing the man in relation to his thought, I, for one, am struck by his controlling concerns, concerns essential, I believe, to understanding man and thought. Two of them, identified by Tillich himself, dominate the course of the first two chapters of our portrait. Tillich describes them as the revolutionary and the romantic motives.

The revolutionary motive represents of course, Tillich's long-standing involvement with the question of authority. In his 1936 description of his life he saw himself on the boundary between "autonomy" and "heteronomy." At that time he indicated that the question of authority had deep ramifications in his life, extending from his early relationship with his father to many of his subsequent theological and political views. Tillich was profoundly opposed to authoritarian patterns of life and thought. His whole interpretation of history is imbued with this antipathy. His reading of history breathes a deep conviction that the human spirit needs freedom, freedom not only from the obvious restrictions of church and state, but freedom also from the less apparent tyranny of past cultural achievements. The "Protestant principle" and the "kairos doctrine" represent Tillich's declaration of freedom against every form of intellectual-spiritual oppression. It was this concern that led him into conflict with Barth in 1923. As previously observed, in that debate Tillich sought to move away from the traditional, "restrictive" doctrines of God and Canon and Church towards what he regarded as the wider, freer sphere of "Spirit." In that debate Tillich declared for a freedom of the present "to create anew out of its own life and in its own words the eternal meaning of all time."[3]

Tillich's anti-authoritarianism found—and I believe will continue to find—a broad, human response. He very much speaks to modern man in these terms. But this is less the case, I think, with the romantic motive. Here one must deal with a somewhat more unique and peculiar concern of Tillich, one which *distinguishes* him *from* rather than *unites* him *with* large numbers of people.

In his rebellion against authoritarian restriction Tillich was not, after all, speaking simply for autonomy. He rejected what he termed "superficial autonomy" and proposed in its stead "theonomy," the distinctive Tillichian term for the realization of a depth of being, an "eternal meaning," within the processes of autonomous cultural creation. Tillich's romantic identification with nature, his sense of participation in the hierarchy of the natural order, may perhaps strike a responsive chord in many, but his romantic-mystical definition of "spiritual depth" within the historical process is especially esoteric. In point of fact not even Tillich exposited systematically and effectively the substance of "theonomy" or "a theology of culture." The *Systematic Theology*, with its method of correlation, attempts something of this task. But Tillich's analyses of "theonomy" within the various spheres of culture are relatively few and, in the opinion of this writer, largely unconvincing as descriptions of "spiritual depth." The subjective, interpretive factor is so

3. See above, p. 58.

dominant in these scattered pieces[4] that they often do not carry along the sympathetic reader, let alone the "unbeliever" who is theoretically the object of this sort of apologetic. In summary, the romantic-mystical base of Tillich's program for reconciling religion and culture, though personally compelling to Tillich himself and an inspiration for much of his thought, posed major problems in communication and greatly restricted his circle of conversants.

Of his revolutionary and romantic concerns, Tillich spoke explicitly. But of a third factor shaping his thought, Tillich spoke less directly—in all probability because he felt it was there for all to see. This was his Christian commitment, the depth of which is especially apparent in the Hirsch affair. I say that this factor becomes especially apparent in the Hirsch affair because in that crisis certain priorities of concern become evident: the revolutionary and romantic motives are accorded subordinate roles. To be sure Tillich's anti-authoritarianism played an important part in his rejection of National Socialism: he insisted that critical protest be maintained in the face of Nazi presumption and distortion. But even more revealing, I think, was Tillich's subtle espousal of certain "heteronomous" patterns of thought that he had previously opposed in debate with Barth. Whereas against Barth he had argued that every "time" ought "to create anew out of its own life . . . the eternal meaning of all time,"

4. In the 1959 book, *Theology of Culture*, (Oxford University Press), Tillich gathered together a number of previously written articles which touched upon varied cultural themes, but this book is hardly to be considered a systematic exposition of the subject.

with Hirsch he insisted that the year 1933 could not be placed on the same level as the year 33 in the history of salvation. And he went on then to make the very important and new distinction between revelation and kairos. Again, in 1923 he had cautioned Barth agaainst being unfaithful to the times and destroying "the bond of fellowship" with those in all areas of culture who struggled for the realization of the spirit of Christ. Yet, later, he declared to Hirsch that the fellowship of the church transcended varying interpretations of the kairos that individual members of the church might hold. And once more—whereas he had earlier spoken of the "Spirit" blowing where it wills, free of the "empty form" of Canon, against Hirsch he affirmed the primary role of "the biblical documents as a source of revelation". These shifts in viewpoint were not, I think, a yielding of ground to Barth—though they can be considered such. Rather, the spontaneity of their statement suggests that they were more likely simply a reflex of faith in the midst of crisis—a "reflex" that was not subsequently forgotten. In his later formulations Tillich took account of the "safeguards" of Christian substance and made room for them as he had not before. This he did even though they introduced obstructions to the easy flow of autonomy and romanticism within the system. Although the Hirsch affair did not lead to revision in the substance of Tillich's Christology, it did prompt him to distinguish more sharply than previously between the first kairos and all secondary kairoi.

A fourth and final factor that I see motivating and inspiring the thought of Tillich is the sheer aesthetic joy of intellectual formulation. There is little that one

175

can cite to support this estimate, but it is the sort of thing that makes a philosopher a philosopher, an artist an artist: a love of order and proportion, a fitting together of things, a resolution of tensions, the challenge of explicating the "inexplicable." This factor pervades, I believe, the whole of Chapters Four and Five of our portrait, the expositions of the ontological frame of reference and the *Systematic Theology*. In these chapters is manifested Tillich's captivation with the mind's capacity to "build a world," a world at times quite independent of the real intractable one. Perhaps this was another reason for Tillich's autobiographical reflections and the frankness of his "confessions": he felt a need to touch the earth, to keep before himself and others the existential truth that life precedes thought. This says, finally, that Tillich was not the existentialist that he claimed to be—or would have liked to have been. I believe this was so. This is why World War I was not quite the intellectual shock to Tillich that it was to some others. This is why, in Tillich's mind, the kairos doctrine and Religious Socialism were so long a-waning: they represented to him what the world should have been rather than what it was. One must note that the coincidence of opposites can, after all, be quite compelling as *logic:* it can perhaps convince the man in doubt that though he does not have faith he believes still in "truth"; perhaps it can even satisfy the man who is sick that though he does not have health he still has life. But really, there *is* a difference between doubt and faith, sickness and health. This is to say that the logic of the coincidence of opposites often yields results strange to life. Deep down, I think, Tillich knew this, but the formula fascinated him nonetheless.

It is important, when reading Tillich, to be aware of these four specific concerns. They were spurs to his thought. And the reconciliation of their separate "demands" constitutes a partial explanation of the complexity and ambiguity of his formulations. Their identification helps the reader understand in part the nature of Tillich's appeal. He speaks to many people at different levels of experience and provides, as it were, "something for everyone." In reading him, one can come to understand better the nature of one's own thought processes just as in viewing a portrait one is often reminded of the qualities of the self.

We cannot, however, stop here in our postscript. As has been stated, Tillich awaited the judgment of the church regarding the system that he had fashioned. It is only right therefore to say a few concluding words about this system that the church must judge.

There is, of course, that large element in Tillich's thought that first brought him fame—his philosophy of history. This aspect of his system, despite its Religious-Socialist failure, is likely to prove most enduring. The "Protestant principle" and the "kairos doctrine," as already indicated, find a wide base in human experience. They lay bare not only the pretension of man but paradoxically appeal to each generation's boredom with all that has gone before. This philosophy of history is, I believe, essentially separable from specifically Christian faith. It finds its roots in Marx and Jewish prophecy and the ontology of creativity. Christology is fundamentally a secondary consideration in its statement. Though Tillich may have sought to correct this deficiency by means of additions and corrections in structural definitions, in the final analysis the "content" of the Cross serves basically the purpose of furthering Tillich's interpretation of the process-character of history. Tillich's own Christian commitment is clear, but the Church, which is to weigh these things, must ask itself about the adequacy of the "norm," as Tillich himself expressed it.

Tillich's Christology, of course, has been the center of much criticism already. Karl Barth, George Tavard, Kenneth Hamilton, Robert C. Johnson, along with many others, have variously expressed dissatisfaction with Tillich's understanding of the person and work of Christ. I cannot but agree with much of this criticism; for, however broad Tillich's starting point in ontology, the place that he finally allows for Christ is really too narrow, too restricted. Independent of the revelation in Christ, Tillich is able to assert that "essential humanity includes the union of God and man."[5] This, he says, is a derivative of "the dialectics of the infinite and the finite." As a result of this prior determination Christology itself is reduced to the statement that "essential manhood has appeared under the conditions of existence."[6] In effect Tillich brings the whole of Christology down to a single theory of the atonement, the moral exemplar theory. On this point the New Testament and church history permit a much wider expression of faith. This the church must surely consider.

In Tillich's translation of Christian faith there are,

5. See above, p. 160.
6. *Ibid.*

to be sure, numerous other problems which have been cited by theological critics, for example, his pantheism, his gnosticism, etc., but I would conclude with a problem arising uniquely from this particular study. It is brought into focus by Tillich's shift in thought from the earlier concentration upon the corporate-historical aspects of existence to the later emphasis upon individualistic motifs. It can be described as the bifurcation of faith and, to my mind, the frustration of a Christian style of life.

The point of origin of this problem is Tillich's "ontological" definition of God derived from Boehme and Schelling, the idea that God must be viewed as a synthesis rather than a thesis. As developed by Schelling and Tillich, this definition of God gives rise to the suspicion that it was first and foremost an intellectual construct designed to resolve ontological problems. At most it can be asseverated as an "intuition" by the microcosm (man) about the macrocosm (Being-Itself). Be this as it may, deity is here represented as the containment of essence and existence, potentiality and actuality, the ground of the "ought-to-be" and the "is." As long as this dualism is balanced and "externalized" in God, or in the corporate-historical reality (where Tillich gave it a "kairos-logos" designation), it perhaps remained tolerable as a theoretical formulation. But when the polarity is "subjectivized" by Tillich, when it passes over into "polar tension" and imbalance *within* the life of faith, it becomes, I submit, insupportable as the basis of a Christian style of life. Simply put, this is to assert that however satisfying Tillich's system may be "aesthetically," *in sum*—and not just here and there and accidentally—it fails to structure Christian life. To use one of Tillich's own terms it fails a "Gestalt" character.

Writing in *Dynamics of Faith*, Tillich declares:

> . . . one can distinguish two main elements in every experience of the holy. One element is the presence of the holy here and now. It consecrates the place and the reality of its appearance. It grasps the mind with terrifying and fascinating power. . . . The holy must be present and felt as present in order to be experienced at all.
>
> At the same time the holy is the judgment over everything that is. It demands personal and social holiness in the sense of justice and love. Our ultimate concern represents what we essentially are and—therefore—ought to be. It stands as the law of our being, against us and for us. Holiness cannot be experienced without its power to command what we should be.
>
> If we call the first element in the experience of the holy the holiness of being, the second element in the experience of the holy could be called the holiness of what ought to be.[7]

In Tillich's exposition, however, these two elements become separated in the life of faith—or better, one gains dominance over the other; for, as Tillich observes, "man is finite and he can never unite all ele-

7. Tillich, *Dynamics of Faith*, (New York: Harper Torchbooks, 1958), p. 56.

ments of truth in complete balance."[8] Because of this, two different types of faith emerge, one in which the holy "is" predominates (the "sacramental-mystical" type of faith) and the other in which the holy "ought-to-be" is dominant (the "prophetic-moral" type). It therefore becomes incumbent upon the individiual to seek to correct the imbalance and supplement one element of faith with the other. Man, Tillich declares, "cannot rest on the awareness of his finitude because faith is concerned with the ultimate and *its adequate expression*."[9] Not only the individual, but Christianity as a whole must "regain in real experience the unity of the divergent types of faith" if it is to "express its claim to answer the questions and to fulfill the dynamics of the history of faith in the past and future."[10]

What frustrates a "style of life" in this analysis is not only the fact that faith is turned in upon itself (Tillich calls it the "dynamics of faith"), but the essential character of the sacramental-mystical type of faith is left largely undefined. It can be assumed on the basis of the *Systematic Theology* and Tillich's formal Christology that "Jesus as the Christ" represents the criterion of the "ought-to-be" since he manifests "essential humanity;" but apart from a comprehensive enjoinment of idolatry no such norm governs the experience of the holy "is." Actually it is at this point that Tillich makes room in the life of faith, not only for the whole tradition of mysticism, Christian

8. *Ibid.*, p. 57.
9. *Ibid.*, p. 57. Italics mine.
10. *Ibid.*, p. 73.

and non-Christian, but also for the important "pan-
theistic element" that he insisted should be part of a
Christian doctrine of God.[11]

Understandably Tillich was sensitive to this "turning in" of faith upon itself and attempted to check its
paralyzing effects in two ways. In the first instance
he restricted the analytic function: " . . . theoretical
isolation . . . is the way to the definition of faith as
ultimate concern. But the life of faith itself does not
include such analytic work."[12] This tends to contradict another assertion of Tillich that faith ". . . is the
centered movement of the *whole personality* toward
something of ultimate meaning and significance."[13] In
the second place, he sought to stay faith's introversion
by insisting that, as "ultimate concern," faith ". . . is
never experienced in isolation from a concrete content."[14] Thus faith must bear the "risk" of idolatry;
it must arm itself with courage. Tillich observes:
"Courage is that element in faith which is related to

11. *Systematic Theology*, I, 233–34. Cf. George F. Mc-
Lean's analysis of Tillich's pantheism in Thomas A. O'Meara
and Celestin D. Weisser's (eds.) *Paul Tillich in Catholic
Thought.* (Dubuque: The Priory Press, 1964), pp. 78–80.
In D. Mackenzie Brown's *Ultimate Concern: Tillich in
Dialogue* Tillich remarks that it is possible to experience
"ultimacy" through "a child, or a flower, or a mountain. It
has happened to me innumerable times through the ocean.
It is not the ocean in its empirical reality, but its transparency
to the infinite, that makes it great." (New York: Harper
& Row, 1965) p. 65.

12. *Dynamics of Faith*, p. 103.

13. *Ibid.*, p. 106. Italics mine. Certainly analytic work is
part of the "whole personality."

14. *Ibid.*, p. 103.

182

the risk of faith. One cannot replace faith by courage, but neither can one describe faith without courage."[15]

This description, I suggest, yields the final despair of "a style of life." Every man must take the risk of a concrete concern and calls upon courage to do so. Courage here is clearly *man's* capacity to affirm himself "in spite of" everything that may obstruct this affirmation. Yet by affirming Jesus as the Christ the individual is assured that "in the picture of the Christ the criterion against its idolatrous abuse is given—the cross."[16] One is forced to conclude that for the Christian the risk of idolatry (and self-destruction) is less great than it would be with other concrete concerns, that therefore less courage is required for this particular expression of faith. In fact Tillich says: "Out of this criterion [i.e. the cross] comes the message which is the very heart of Christianity and *makes possible the courage to affirm faith* in the Christ, namely, that in spite of all forces of separation between God and man this is overcome from the side of God.[17] In this final assertion courage is *made possible by the message;* and it is difficult to see, under these circumstances, how it is still *man's* "in spite of" that is being described. Indeed, there is introduced at this point a second "in spite of," the "in spite of" of God's grace, which is addressed to man in his sin and that seems to displace courage as a basis of the life of faith. Tillich concludes:

15. *Ibid.*
16. *Ibid.*, p. 104.
17. *Ibid.* Italics mine.

We are never able to bridge the infinite distance between the infinite and the finite from the side of the finite. This alone makes the courage of faith possible. The risk of failure, of error and of idolatrous distortion can be taken, because the failure cannot separate us from what is our ultimate concern.[18]

Not only is courage no longer courage—but the particular message of Christian faith is "universalized" as the substance of the relationship of the infinite and the finite.

The final despair of a style of life is that Tillich's bifurcation of faith passes over into a confusion of courage and grace which robs both of their vital meaning. Tillich's concern for synthesis, his eagerness to speak the words "both-and," bear the cost of eliminating in thought what is real in life, the alternatives of courage and grace as bases for life. No real purpose, I think, is finally served by theoretically denying to man the possibility of living life from his own inner strength in the face of meaninglessness, death, guilt. It appears that, more and more, awareness of this possibility is becoming the mark of the secular man. The secular man lives life without grace, without a sense of transcendent meaning and support in the form either of "Being-Itself" or the God of Israel. And to characterize this pattern of life as "superficial autonomy" is, I suggest, apologetically meaningless and futile. In addition and more importantly, the effort to baptize courage with grace leads on to a

18. *Ibid.*, p. 105.

major dilution of the Gospel. It obscures the central meaning of Jesus' own ministry, that of preaching "good news to the poor . . . ," proclaiming "release to the captives and recovering of sight to the blind," setting "at liberty those who are oppressed . . ." (*Luke 4:18*). Besides declaring that "there is none good, but . . . God" (*Matt. 19:17*), words of Jesus much stressed by Tillich, the New Testament makes clear that "the righteous" have no need of a saviour (*cf. Matt. 9:10–13*). In the end the question comes down to this: does the New Testament principally, and not secondarily, articulate a choice in way of life? To believe that it does forces one to recognize alternatives rather than "polarities." On the other hand and by contrast, the urge to synthesize tends only to eliminate the tension of choice and in Tillich's thought confuses courage and grace.

In considering this particular feature of Tillich's thought, the question whether it yields a distinctive Christian "piety," the Church would do well to remind itself that "courage" as a concept, a way of life, does not appear in the New Testament. This is not because the word and the concept were not then known; Tillich himself reminds us that the Greeks knew all about courage. Rather, it is because the writers of the New Testament understood that when speaking about grace one simply does not also speak about courage.

Tillich's "system," as already suggested, will undoubtedly bear its enduring elements. Many in the future—as they do today—will find his thought stimulating, enlightening, challenging. The Christian cer-

185

tainly will find instruction here. But the whole, from this viewing, is not equal to some of its parts. Tillich, the man, held it all together—and it is my surmise that future students of the system will inevitably come back to ask about the man. This portrait suggests that we cannot have one without the other.

# INDEX

Abyss, concept of the, 30, 42, 50
Aristotle, 112
Augustine, 56, 107 ff.
Autonomy, 24, 45 f., 115 f., 119, 172 f.

Baader, F., 169
Barth, K., 12, 13, 17, 18, 34, 35–64, 65, 70, 71, 78, 79 f., 88, 90, 157, 168, 172, 173 f., 178
Being/Being-itself, 107, 119 f., 130, 132 f., 134, 155, 158, 179, 184; ground of, 42, 50, 123, 144, 158
Boehme, J., 169, 179
Bonhoeffer, D., 12
Bruno, G., 109

Christ, 28, 41, 48, 49, 54 ff., 58, 59 ff., 63, 122 ff., 156 ff., 159 ff., 166, 175, 178, 181, 183
Church, the, 40, 53, 56, 59, 61, 92 ff., 106 f., 171, 177 f.
Coincidence of opposites, 27, 41 f., 112 f., 123, 133, 160, 176
Confessing Church, 90
Courage, 182 ff.
Creation, 42 ff., 147 ff.
Cusanus, N., 109, 112

Demonic, the, 67 f.
Descartes, R., 108

Dialectical Theology. *See* Neo-orthodoxy
Dialectics, 40 ff., 52, 133
Dionysius, 130
Doubt, 26 f., 100, 134

Eschatology, 78 ff.
Essence/essentialization, 151 ff., 161
Existentialism, 82 ff., 98 ff., 167

Faith, 26 f., 50, 134, 155, 180 ff.
Fall, the, 150 f.
Feuerbach, L., 76
Fichte, J. G., 25, 169
Finitude, 123, 126, 144, 156, 158 ff.
Freedom, 115 f., 119, 121, 136 f., 144, 147, 151 f., 158, 163, 165 f.

German Christians, the, 70, 75, 89 f.
Gestalt, 142 ff., 166, 180
God, 28, 40 ff., 53 f., 55, 58, 59, 63, 79, 110 ff., 119–26, 130, 134 f., 148 ff., 155, 179, 182; word of, 37
Goethe, J. W., 43
Gogarten, F., 39, 42, 43 ff., 50 ff., 56, 59, 70, 75
Grace, 158, 183 ff.
Grasping function, 142 ff., 152

187

Hamilton, K., 178
Harnack, A., 16, 107
Hegel, G. F. W., 25, 62, 76, 106 f., 130, 168, 169
Heidegger, M., 76, 83, 84, 96, 98 f.
Heimann, E., 32
Herberger, K., 38
Herrmann, W., 107
Heteronomy, 49, 58, 121, 172
Hirsch, E., 12, 44, 69–89, 157, 174 f.
Hitler, A., 68, 69, 86
Holy Spirit/Spirit, 44, 53, 59, 60 f., 123, 125, 163, 166
Hume, D., 113 f.

Identity, principle of, 25 f., 107 ff., 114 f., 129

Jaspers, K., 76, 83 f., 96, 98 f.
Jesus, 27 f., 49, 56, 58, 78, 160 f.
Johnson, R. C., 139, 157, 178
Justification by faith, 26, 100

Kaehler, M., 26, 28
Kaftan, J., 107
Kairos, 11, 13, 32 ff., 51 f., 57 f., 67, 74 f., 77 f., 85 ff., 95, 97 ff., 101, 126, 148, 172, 175, 176, 177
Kant, I., 25, 38, 113–18, 140 ff., 154
Kierkegaard, S., 38, 75, 83, 98, 111, 113

Leibniz, G. W., 109 f., 112
Locke, J., 113

McLean, G. F., 182
Malebranche, N., 108 f.
Martin, B., 84
Marx, K./Marxism, 31, 32, 75, 76, 83, 98, 147, 168, 169, 177
Method of correlation, 17, 87, 137 ff.
Microcosm, 100, 109 f., 179

National Socialism/Nazism, 68, 71, 82, 85, 90, 91, 174
Neo-orthodoxy, 17, 65, 79, 90, 168
New Being, 97 ff., 100, 102, 159 ff., 167
Niebuhr, H. R., 68
Niebuhr, Reinhold, 68, 150
Nietzsche, F., 31, 164, 168, 169

One/Many, 107 ff., 144, 165
Ontology, 97 f., 101–26, 128 ff.
Otto, R., 16

Pauck, W., 168
Philosophy, 137 ff., 146, 155
Plato, 38, 108, 112, 130
Plotinus, 108, 112, 130
Polarity, principle of, 133 ff., 138, 145 f.
Protestant principle, 33, 36, 154, 172, 177
Psychology, depth, 96, 99

Reason, 140 f.; depth of, 46; subjective, 142
Religious socialism, 13, 31 ff., 35 f., 69, 72–100, 104, 148, 153, 166 f., 176
Revelation, 46, 48, 54, 59 f., 85 ff., 121 f., 175; natural, 91
Revolutionary motif, 11, 25, 26, 172 f.
Roman Catholic Church, 91
Romanticism, 19 ff., 25, 173 f.

Sartre, J. P., 96, 99
Schelling, F., 20 f., 25, 28 f., 30 f., 41, 79, 83, 104–26, 127 f.,

188

133, 134, 140, 149, 150, 154, 156, 158, 161 f., 167 ff., 179
Schleiermacher, F., 16, 25, 62, 169
Schmidt, K. L., 39
Shaping function, 142 ff., 152
Sin, 111, 122–25, 159, 166
Socrates, 108
Spinoza, 110, 115
Stapel, W., 89
Subject-object cleavage, 28, 79, 108 f., 129, 137, 144, 165

Tavard, G. F., 15, 39, 97 ff., 161, 178
Theology, 137 ff., 146, 155
Theonomy, 33, 56, 173
Thomas, J. H., 39, 84
Torrance, T. F., 39
Troeltsch, E., 16, 38 f., 103, 168

Ultimate concern, 155, 167, 182
Unconditional, the, 40 ff., 50, 52 f., 59, 63, 79
Utopianism, 82

189